The Alchemy of Vision

Exploring The Depths of Heaven and Hell Through William Blake and Neville Goddard

By

Mychael T. Renn

Copyright © 2023

All Rights Reserved

I AM

"If fool there be,

Then I am he

To claim another, I than "ME,"

For I AM ALL THE I I SEE,

THE ONLY I THAT I CAN BE,

THE I-AM-ALL, INFINITY---

Then who or what

Can trouble ME?"

- Alfred Aiken

Contents

Preface 6

Chapter One Understanding William Blake's 'The Marriage of Heaven and Hell' 1

   Part One: An Introduction to William Blake and 'The Marriage of Heaven and Hell 1

   "The Marriage of Heaven and Hell" through Goddard's Lens ... 5

      THE ARGUMENT 5

   Navigating "The Voice of the Devil" through Goddard's Perception 10

      THE VOICE OF THE DEVIL 10

      A MEMORABLE FANCY (1) 15

      A MEMORABLE FANCY (2) 20

      A MEMORABLE FANCY (3) 24

      A MEMORABLE FANCY (4) 32

Chapter Two Introduction to Neville Goddard's Core Teachings 37

   Part One: Laying the Foundation from Mystic to Modern Guide 37

   Part Two: The Power of Imagination in Neville Goddard's Teachings 40

   Part Three: Alignment with Blake's Visionary Concepts 43

   Part Four: Practical Applications of Goddard's Teachings 46

   Part Five: The Transformative Power of Imagination and Consciousness 50

Chapter Three Exploring the Union of Reason and Imagination . 54

    Part One: Neville Goddard's Interpretation of "The Marriage of Heaven and Hell" 54

    Part Two: The Profound Understanding of Spiritual Truth 58

Chapter Four Applying Neville Goddard's Principles to Personal Growth 61

    Part One: Unleashing the Creative Powers Within 61

    Part Two: Practical Techniques for Enhancing Imagination and Consciousness 65

    Part Three: Integrating Practices into Daily Life for Manifestation and Spiritual Growth 69

Chapter 5: Unveiling the Mysteries in Paradoxes 73

Introduction to Proverbs 76

Proverbs of Hell 80

Acknowledgment 222

About The Author 224

Preface

In the realm of visionary thinkers and spiritual pioneers, the works of William Blake and Neville Goddard stand as beacons of profound insight and transformative wisdom. Both Blake's "The Marriage of Heaven and Hell" and Goddard's teachings on imagination and consciousness invite us to explore the depths of our existence and challenge conventional perspectives on spirituality.

This book serves as a harmonious union between these two visionary minds, delving into the rich tapestry of Blake's work through the lens of Goddard's teachings. By intertwining their visionary insights, we embark on a journey of exploration and self-discovery, inviting us to reconsider the nature of heaven, hell, reason, imagination, and the limitless potential of human consciousness.

In the following chapters, we will embark on an intellectual and spiritual adventure guided by the wisdom of William Blake and the transformative teachings of Neville Goddard. We will unravel the profound symbolism within Blake's "The Marriage of Heaven and Hell" while simultaneously unveiling the remarkable connections to Goddard's principles of imagination and conscious creation.

This book is not a mere scholarly analysis or a compendium of esoteric concepts. It is a heartfelt invitation to engage with these visionary perspectives on a personal level, to integrate their wisdom into our lives, and to embark on a transformative journey of self-discovery and spiritual growth.

As you delve into the chapters that follow, I encourage you to approach this exploration with an open mind and a willingness to question long-held beliefs. Prepare to venture beyond the boundaries of conventional wisdom and embrace the paradoxes and mysteries that lie within the marriage of heaven and hell.

May this book serve as a guide, igniting the sparks of insight and inspiration within you. May it illuminate new pathways of understanding and empower you to harness the creative power of your own consciousness.

Welcome to The Alchemy of Vision with—William Blake and Neville Goddard—as we embark on a transformative journey through the realms of heaven and hell.

Chapter One
Understanding William Blake's 'The Marriage of Heaven and Hell'

Part One: An Introduction to William Blake and 'The Marriage of Heaven and Hell

The Enigma That Was William Blake

Stepping into the world of William Blake is akin to entering a realm where boundaries blur between the spiritual and the tangible, the esoteric and the evident. Born in the latter half of the 18th century, Blake was not just a poet or an artist; he was a visionary, a revolutionary who often walked the tightrope between genius and heresy.

Growing up in a turbulent era marked by the stirrings of the Industrial Revolution and socio-political upheavals, Blake developed a fierce individualism. His perspectives, though rooted in his times, often transcended them, challenging established norms and venturing into uncharted territories of thought and belief.

Unveiling "The Marriage of Heaven and Hell"

Amidst the vast corpus of Blake's work, "The Marriage of Heaven and Hell" stands as a beacon of his radical philosophy and vibrant imagination. Composed between 1790 and 1793, this prose piece is an intricate tapestry of poetry, parable, and aphorism infused with vivid illustrations.

On the surface, it may seem like a diatribe against organized religion and conventional morality. However, delving deeper reveals that it's an audacious exploration of the dualities of existence—good and evil, heaven and hell, reason and energy.

Challenging Established Dogmas

One of the profound aspects of this work is Blake's criticism of conventional religious teachings. He challenges the age-old dichotomies set by traditional dogmas, arguing against the compartmentalization of good and evil. For Blake, heaven and hell weren't distant realms but interwoven aspects of human experience.

"The Marriage of Heaven and Hell" serves as a manifesto where Blake articulates his belief in the inherent divinity of humanity. Rejecting the orthodox portrayal of a vengeful God and eternal damnation, he propounds a view where hell is not a place of torment but a source of primal energy and creativity.

The Proverbs of Hell

A significant segment of the text is the 'Proverbs of Hell.' These aphorisms, though seemingly paradoxical, encapsulate Blake's revolutionary ideas. Phrases like "The road of excess leads to the palace of wisdom" challenge conventional wisdom, urging readers to question established norms and to recognize the sanctity in what's traditionally considered sinful or profane.

A Fusion of Art and Text

Integral to understanding "The Marriage of Heaven and Hell" is the recognition of Blake's unique method of 'illuminated printing.' His fusion of handcrafted text with intricate illustrations brings forth an immersive experience. Each plate is not just a page but a canvas where words and images dance in a harmonious ballet, lending layers of meaning to the narrative.

Concluding Thoughts on the Introduction

As we embark on this exploration of Blake's work", it's vital to approach it not as a mere literary artifact but as a portal—a gateway into the profound depths of Blake's visionary universe. It beckons us to challenge our preconceived notions, to embrace paradoxes, and to recognize the sacred union of opposites within ourselves.

MYCHAEL T. RENN

In the chapters that follow, we'll dissect the intricate layers of this masterpiece, journeying through its themes, symbolism, and profound impact, all the while seeking to understand its harmonious connection to Neville Goddard's teachings.

The Alchemy of Vision

"The Marriage of Heaven and Hell" through Goddard's Lens

THE ARGUMENT

RINTRAH roars and shakes his fires in the burden's air,

Hungry clouds swag on the deep.

Once meek, and in a perilous path

The just man kept his course along

MYCHAEL T. RENN

The Vale of Death.

Roses are planted where thorns grow,

And on the barren heath

Sing the honey bees.

Then, the perilous path was planted,

And a river and a spring

On every cliff and tomb

And on the bleached bones

Red clay brought forth:

Till the villain left the paths of ease

To walk in perilous paths, and drive

The just man into barren climes.

Now the sneaking serpent walks

In mild humility;

And the just man rages in the wilds

Where lions roam.

Rintrah roars and shakes his fires in the   burden's air,

Hungry clouds swag on the deep.

As a new heaven is begun, and it is now thirty-three years

The Alchemy of Vision

since its advent, the Eternal Hell revives. And lo! Swedenborg is the angel sitting at the tomb: his writings are the linen clothes folded up. Now is the dominion of Edom and the return of Adam into Paradise.—See Isaiah xxxiv. and xxxv. chap. Without contraries is no progression. Attraction and repulsion, reason and energy, love, and hate are necessary to human existence.

From these contraries spring what the religious call Good and Evil. Good is the passive that obeys reason; Evil is the active springing from Energy.

Good is heaven. Evil is hell.

Introduction:

"The Argument" sets the stage for the themes Blake explores throughout "The Marriage of Heaven and Hell." The juxtaposition of contraries, the role of energy and reason, and the balance between good and evil lay the foundation. Neville Goddard's teachings can offer a unique lens through which to view these concepts, bridging the spiritual with the practical.

Context Setting:

Blake introduces Rintrah, a figure that embodies wrath and passion, shaking the skies with his fiery roars. The poem depicts a landscape undergoing transformation, where once barren and perilous paths bloom with roses and streams, hinting at redemption and rebirth.

Analysis:

- Rintrah and the Landscape: In Goddard's teachings, our imagination and feelings are the causes of the circumstances of our lives. The transformation of the landscape from perilous to abundant might be seen as an allegory for the transformative power of imagination and belief.

- "Roses are planted where thorns grow": Goddard often spoke about the transformative power of positive thinking and belief. This line echoes the idea that even in adversity, with the right mindset (or 'imagination' in Goddard's terms), one can find growth and beauty.

- "Now the sneaking serpent walks / In mild humility; / And the just man rages in the wilds / Where lions roam": This contrasts the idea of the 'meek' who have now found power and the 'just' who now wander lost. Goddard might interpret this as a shift in consciousness, where those who awaken to the power of their imagination (serpent) can manifest their desires, while those bound by societal norms (just man) feel trapped.

Context Setting:

Blake presents a new heaven and alludes to the idea that without opposition or "contraries," there is no progression. He labels "Good" as passive obedience to reason and "Evil" as active energy.

The Alchemy of Vision

Analysis:

- "Without contraries is no progression." Goddard emphasized that desires or wishes often arise from moments of contrast or opposition in our lives. It is in these moments of wanting, born from contrast, that we harness the imaginative power to create.

- "Attraction and repulsion, reason and energy, love, and hate, are necessary to human existence." This highlights the dual nature of existence. Goddard would likely agree, emphasizing that understanding these dualities allows us to better harness our imaginative powers. Recognizing the balance of these forces is key to manifesting our desires.

- "Good is the passive that obeys reason; Evil is the active springing from Energy. ": This is an interesting delineation, as Goddard viewed imagination and feeling (which can be equated to Blake's 'energy') as paramount to manifesting one's desires. In a sense, the 'evil' or 'energy' Blake refers to might be what Goddard sees as the driving force of creation.

Conclusion:

Both Blake and Goddard recognize the essential nature of dualities in human experience. While their language and approach differ, at their core, they both highlight the transformative power of understanding and embracing these dualities. The active energy or imagination that Blake and Goddard refer to, respectively, serves as the catalyst for change and creation in our lives.

MYCHAEL T. RENN

Navigating "The Voice of the Devil" through Goddard's Perception

THE VOICE OF THE DEVIL

All Bibles or sacred codes have been the cause of the following errors:

1. That man has two real existing principles, viz., a Body and a Soul.
2. That Energy, called Evil, is alone from the Body; and that

Reason, called Good, is alone from the Soul.
3. That God will torment man in Eternity for following his Energies.

But the following contraries to these are true:

1. Man has no Body distinct from his Soul. For that called Body is a portion of the Soul discerned by the five senses, the chief inlets of the Soul in this age.
2. Energy is the only life and is from the Body, and Reason is the bound or outward circumference of Energy.
3. Energy is an Eternal Delight.

Those who restrain desire do so because theirs is weak enough to be restrained, and the restrainer or reason usurps its place and governs the unwilling.

And being restrained, it by degrees becomes passive till it is only the shadow of desire.

The history of this is written in Paradise Lost, and the Governor or Reason is called Messiah. The original Archangel or possessor of the command of the heavenly host is called the Devil, or Satan, and his children are called Sin and Death. But in the book of Job, Milton's Messiah is called Satan. For this, history has been adopted by both parties.

It indeed appeared to Reason as if the desire was cast out,

but the Devil's account is that the Messiah fell and formed a heaven of what he stole from the abyss.

This is shown in the Gospel, where he prays to the Father to send the Comforter or desire that Reason may have ideas to build on, the Jehovah of the Bible being no other than he who dwells in flaming fire. Know that after Christ's death, he became Jehovah.

But in Milton, the Father is Destiny, the Son a ratio of the five senses, and the Holy Ghost vacuum!

Note: The reason Milton wrote in fetters when he wrote of Angels and God and at Liberty when of Devils and Hell is because he was a true poet and of the Devil's party without knowing it.

Introduction:

"The Voice of the Devil" challenges foundational beliefs deeply ingrained in religious and societal doctrine. By juxtaposing traditional teachings with his revolutionary ideas, Blake ignites a dialogue on the nature of desire, reason, and self-imposed boundaries. When we overlay Neville Goddard's philosophies on this, an enriched understanding emerges.

Context Setting:

Blake seeks to overturn the long-standing dualities: body and soul, good and evil, reason and energy. He engages in a powerful

The Alchemy of Vision

discourse that reframes our understanding of these dualities, thus offering a broader perception of human nature and divinity.

Analysis:

- "That man has two real existing principles, viz., a Body and a Soul." vs. "Man has no Body distinct from his Soul. ": Blake's assertion resonates with Goddard's view that our physical reality is shaped by our consciousness. There isn't a clear demarcation; instead, the external (body) mirrors the internal (soul/consciousness).

- "Energy, called Evil, is alone from the Body; and that Reason, called Good, is alone from the Soul." vs. "Energy is the only life, and is from the Body, and Reason is the bound or outward circumference of Energy. ": Goddard would perceive 'Energy' as the imaginative force, the very essence that gives life to our desires. Reason, while essential, can limit this force if it becomes the dominant factor. It's about balancing imaginative energy with rationality.

- "Energy is Eternal Delight. ": This aligns perfectly with Goddard's teachings. Passion, joy, and desire are the cornerstones of our imaginative power. To live in one's desired state of consciousness is indeed an eternal delight.

- "Those who restrain desire do so because theirs is weak enough to be restrained, and the restrainer or reason usurps its place and governs the unwilling.   ": This is reminiscent of Goddard's idea that if one's desire is genuine and passionate, it should be pursued without restraint. True desires, according to Goddard, stem from our higher self and thus should be embraced, not suppressed.

- The references to Paradise Lost, Messiah, the Devil, and Satan   : These allude to the eternal battle between desire and reason. Goddard might interpret this as the inner conflicts one faces when trying to manifest desires. Sometimes, societal "reason" suppresses genuine desires, leading to a life unfulfilled.

- Note about Milton   : Blake's observation that Milton wrote more freely about Devils and Hell can be linked to Goddard's idea of freeing oneself from societal constraints to truly manifest one's desires. Sometimes, stepping outside conventional beliefs leads to a richer, fuller life.

Conclusion:

"The Voice of the Devil" is not just a challenge to conventional beliefs but an invitation to see beyond them. With insights from Neville Goddard, one realizes the true potential of imaginative energy and the importance of embracing genuine desires.

The Alchemy of Vision

A MEMORABLE FANCY (1)

The Prophets Isaiah and Ezekiel dined with me, and I asked them how they dared so roundly to assert that God spoke to them and whether they did not think at the time that they would be misunderstood and so be the cause of imposition.

Isaiah answered: "I saw no God, nor heard any, in a finite organical perception: but my senses discovered the infinite in everything; and as I was then persuaded, and remained confirmed, that the voice of honest indignation is the voice of God, I cared not for consequences, but wrote."

Then I asked: "Does a firm persuasion that a thing is so make it so?"

He replied: "All poets believe that it does, and in ages of imagination, this firm persuasion removed mountains, but many are not capable of a firm persuasion of anything."

Then Ezekiel said: "The philosophy of the East taught the first principles of human perception; some nations held one principle for the origin and some another. We of Israel taught that the Poetic Genius (as you now call it) was the first principle and all the others merely derivative, which was the cause of our despising the Priests and Philosophers of other countries and prophesying that all Gods would at last be proved to originate in ours and to be the tributaries of the Poetic Genius. It was this that our great poet King David desired so fervently and invoked so pathetically, saying by this he conquers enemies and governs kingdoms; and we so loved our God that we cursed in His name all the deities of surrounding nations, and asserted that they had rebelled. From these opinions, the vulgar came to think that all nations would at last be subject to the Jews.

"This," said he, "like all firm persuasions, is come to pass, for all nations believe the Jews' code and worship the Jews' God; and what greater subjection can be?"

The Alchemy of Vision

I heard this with some wonder and must confess my own conviction. After dinner, I asked Isaiah to favor the world with his lost works; he said none of the equal value was lost. Ezekiel said the same to him.

I also asked Isaiah what made him go naked and barefoot for three years. He answered: "The same that made our friend Diogenes the Grecian."

I then asked Ezekiel why he ate dung and lay so long on his right and left side. He answered: "The desire of raising other men into a perception of the infinite. This is the North American tribe's practice. And is he honest who resists his genius or conscience, only for the sake of present ease or gratification?"

Introduction:

"A Memorable Fancy" showcases Blake's visionary interaction with the Prophets Isaiah and Ezekiel. They discuss the nature of God, the power of belief, and the sacrifices one makes for a higher calling. Given the deeply spiritual themes, integrating Neville Goddard's principles will add depth and dimension to its interpretation.

Context Setting:

Blake brings to light challenging dialogues that revolve around divine revelations, the influence of firm beliefs, and the idea of the Poetic Genius as the supreme guiding principle. He probes the motivations behind extreme actions taken by prophets for their faith.

Analysis:

- Isaiah's Revelation : Isaiah speaks of perceiving the infinite in everything and expressing the voice of honest indignation. This aligns with Goddard's teachings on the importance of feeling and believing in the end result. For Goddard, "feeling is the secret." The deeper the feeling, the more real the manifestation becomes in our reality.

- "Does a firm persuasion that a thing is so make it so? ": One of the most Goddard-esque ideas presented. For Goddard, belief in an idea or state until it hardens into fact is the cornerstone of manifestation. When Isaiah replies about poets believing it does, it's reminiscent of Goddard's teaching that imagination creates reality.

- Ezekiel on the Poetic Genius : By stating that Poetic Genius is the first principle from which all other principles derive, Ezekiel emphasizes the importance of imaginative creation. This idea mirrors Goddard's philosophy, where imagination is the divine body in each of us.

- "Is he honest who resists his genius or conscience, only for the sake of present ease or gratification? ": A profound reflection on the value of short-term comfort vs. long-term spiritual insight. Through a Goddardian lens, this resonates with the idea of living in the end, with complete fidelity to one's desires, even if it means sacrificing immediate comfort.

Conclusion:

"A Memorable Fancy" is a testament to the power of belief, the omnipresence of the divine, and the sacrifices made in the name of spiritual truths. The dialogues with the prophets emphasize the significance of strong convictions and the transformative power they wield. Through the teachings of Neville Goddard, we understand that the potency of such convictions lies in their ability to shape our reality, guiding us toward greater enlightenment and realization.

MYCHAEL T. RENN

A MEMORABLE FANCY (2)

I was in a printing-house in Hell and saw the method by which knowledge is transmitted from generation to generation.

In the first chamber was a dragon-man, clearing away the rubbish from a cave's mouth; within, a number of dragons were hollowing the cave.

In the second chamber was a viper folding round the rock and the cave, and others adorning it with gold, silver, and precious stones.

The Alchemy of Vision

In the third chamber was an eagle with wings and feathers of air; he caused the inside of the cave to be infinite; around were numbers of eagle-like men who built palaces in the immense cliffs.

In the fourth chamber were lions of flaming fire raging around and melting the metals into living fluids.

In the fifth chamber were unnamed forms, which cast the metals into the expanse.

There, they were received by men who occupied the sixth chamber and took the forms of books and were arranged in libraries.

Introduction:

In this piece, Blake vividly describes a printing house in Hell, illustrating the transmission of knowledge across generations. Through the series of chambers, he introduces a system that transforms raw matter into structured knowledge, hinting at deeper spiritual processes. This allegory can be enhanced with Neville Goddard's teachings on creation, belief, and manifestation.

Context Setting:

Blake uses powerful imagery of mythical creatures and elemental forces, transforming chaos into order, which metaphorically represents the creation process. This narrative captures the journey from raw, unrefined ideas to structured knowledge.

Analysis:

- First and Second Chambers : The dragons and viper depict the initial stages of creation—clearing away chaos and beginning to give it form. Through Goddard's lens, this can be seen as the first inkling of a desire or the initial visualization of a manifestation.

- Third and Fourth Chambers : Eagles, representing infinite possibilities, and lions, embodying fiery passion, indicate the next stages. This is reminiscent of Goddard's teaching of feeling the wish fulfilled, instilling the desire with passion and life.

- Fifth and Sixth Chambers : Transition from undefined forms to structured knowledge in the form of books. Goddard would see this as the final manifestation—the realization of a desire in the physical realm, solidified by belief and assumption.

- The Giants and Chains : This concept is reminiscent of Goddard's teachings about limiting beliefs. The "chains" symbolize self-imposed limitations, while the giants represent our boundless potential.

- Prolific vs. Devouring : This duality mirrors Goddard's idea of our dual nature—the imaginative, creative self and the self that is bound by sensory evidence. The balance between creation and consumption is essential for the flow of life.

- "God only acts and is in existing beings or men. ": This aligns perfectly with Goddard's belief that God is our imagination and that we are the operant powers bringing our desires to life.

- Reconciliation vs. Separation : The assertion that these two forces should be enemies and not reconciled might seem contrary to Goddard's teachings. However, considering it deeper, Goddard often spoke of the need to remain faithful to one's imaginative act and not let doubts (or the devouring) consume it.

Conclusion:

Blake's portrayal of the printing house in Hell offers a metaphorical journey of creation, from chaos to order. Through Neville Goddard's teachings, we appreciate this as an allegory of the manifestation process. The journey from a mere desire, imbued with passion and feeling, finally manifesting in the physical realm, emphasizes the divine creative power within us.

MYCHAEL T. RENN

A MEMORABLE FANCY (3)

An Angel came to me and said: "O pitiable foolish young man! O horrible, O dreadful state! Consider the hot burning dungeon thou art preparing for thyself to all Eternity, to which thou art going in such career."

I said: "Perhaps you will be willing to show me my eternal lot, and we will contemplate together upon it and see whether your lot or mine is most desirable."

So he took me through a stable, and through a church, and

The Alchemy of Vision

down into the church vault, at the end of which was a mill; through the mill, we went, and came to a cave; down the winding cavern we groped our tedious way, till a void boundless as a nether sky appeared beneath us, and we held by the roots of trees and hung over this immensity; but I said: "If you please, we will commit ourselves to this void, and see whether Providence is here also; if you will not, I will." But he answered: "Do not presume, O young man; but as we here remain, behold thy lot, which will soon appear when the darkness passes away."

So I remained with him, sitting in the twisted root of an oak; he was suspended in a fungus, which hung with the head downward into the deep.

By degrees, we beheld the infinite abyss, fiery as the smoke of a burning city; beneath us at an immense distance was the sun, black but shining; round it were fiery tracks on which revolved vast spiders, crawling after their prey, which flew, or rather swum, in the infinite deep, in the most terrific shapes of animals sprung from corruption; and the air was full of them, and seemed composed of them. These are Devils and are called powers of the air. I now asked my companion, which was my eternal lot. He said: "Between the black and white spiders."

The Alchemy of Vision

But now, from between the black and white spiders, a cloud and fire burst and rolled through the deep, blackening all beneath so that the nether deep grew black as a sea and rolled with a terrible noise. Beneath us was nothing now to be seen but a black tempest, till looking East between the clouds and the waves, we saw a cataract of blood mixed with fire, and not many stones' throw from us appeared and sunk again the scaly fold of a monstrous serpent. At last, to the East, distant about three degrees, appeared a fiery crest above the waves; slowly, it reared like a ridge of golden rocks till we discovered two globes of crimson fire, from which the sea fled away in clouds of smoke; and now we saw it was the head of Leviathan. His forehead was divided into streaks of green and purple, like those on a tiger's forehead; soon, we saw his mouth and red gills hang just above the raging foam, tinging the black deeps with beams of blood, advancing toward us with all the fury of spiritual existence.

My friend the Angel climbed up from his station into the mill. I remained alone, and then this appearance was no more, but I found myself sitting on a pleasant bank beside a river by moonlight, hearing a harper who sang to the harp, and his theme was: "The man who never alters his opinion is like standing water, and breeds reptiles of the mind." But I arose and sought for the mill, and there I found my Angel, who, surprised, asked me how I escaped.

I answered: "All that we saw was owing to your

metaphysics, for when you ran away, I found myself on a bank by moonlight, hearing a harper. But now we have seen my eternal lot. Shall I show you yours?" He laughed at my proposal, but I by force suddenly caught him in my arms and flew Westerly through the night till we were elevated above the earth's shadow; then I flung myself with him directly into the body of the sun; here I clothed myself in white, and taking in my hand Swedenborg's volumes, sunk from the glorious clime, and passed all the planets till we came to Saturn. Here, I stayed to rest and then leaped into the void between Saturn and the fixed stars.

"Here," said I, "is your lot; in this space, if space it may be called." Soon, we saw the stable and the church, and I took him to the altar and opened the Bible, and lo! It was a deep pit into which I descended, driving the Angel before me. Soon, we saw seven houses of brick. Once we entered. In it were a number of monkeys, baboons, and all of that species, chained by the middle, grinning and snatching at one another but withheld by the shortness of their chains. However, I saw that they sometimes grew numerous, and then the weak were caught by the strong, and with a grinning aspect, first coupled with and then devoured by plucking off first one limb and then another till the body was left a helpless trunk; this, after grinning and kissing it with seeming fondness, they devoured too. And here and there, I saw one savourily picking the flesh off his own tail. As the stench terribly annoyed us both, we went into the mill, and I, in my hand, brought the skeleton of a body, which in the mill was Aristotle's Analytics.

So the Angel said: "Thy phantasy has imposed upon me, and thou oughtest to be ashamed." I answered: "We impose on one another, and it is but lost time to converse with you whose works are only Analytics."

Introduction:

In "A Memorable Fancy," Blake presents a surreal journey with an Angel, revealing the vast expanse of human consciousness and spiritual states. This rich allegory, filled with symbolic landscapes and creatures, is further deepened when interpreted using Neville Goddard's teachings on the power of imagination and the manifestation of desires.

Context Setting:

Blake's encounter with the Angel symbolizes the eternal tussle between traditional religious beliefs and personal spiritual revelations. This dynamic interaction between external authority and internal realization is at the core of Goddard's teachings.

Analysis:

- Angel's Warning : The initial caution from the Angel echoes society's conventional warnings and restraints. In Goddard's philosophy, these external voices often act as limiting beliefs, obstructing our true imaginative potential.

- The Abyss and Leviathan : The perilous landscapes Blake traverses symbolize the challenges of the human psyche. Goddard would interpret the Leviathan and the abyss as representations of our deepest fears or suppressed desires. Facing these "monsters" is akin to confronting and overcoming our limiting beliefs.

- The Harper's Message : The lesson, "The man who never alters his opinion is like standing water, and breeds reptiles of the mind," is a potent alignment with Goddard's teachings. Holding onto stagnant beliefs can hinder the manifestation process, emphasizing the importance of flexibility and growth in our spiritual journey.

- Sun and Saturn : These celestial symbols encapsulate the vast range of human experiences. The sun, illuminating and warm, is emblematic of spiritual realization, while Saturn, with its connotations of restriction, represents our self-imposed limitations. Goddard believed in transcending such limitations through the power of imagination.

- The Bible and Monkeys : The portrayal of the Bible as a deep pit and the scene with the chained monkeys shed light on the dangers of rigid dogma and unchecked desires. Through Goddard's perspective, these scenarios emphasize the need for personal revelation over external dictates and the careful navigation of our desires.

- Aristotle's Analytics : Blake's depiction of this work as a mere skeleton critiques a life led purely by reason, devoid of imagination or passion. Goddard would concur, emphasizing that while reason has its place, imagination is the primary creative force in our lives.

Conclusion:

Blake's "A Memorable Fancy" delves deep into the spiritual journey of a soul, balancing external dogmas with personal realizations. Interpreted through Neville Goddard's teachings, this chapter underscores the importance of harnessing one's imagination, confronting and transcending fears, and recognizing the divine within. It acts as a beacon, guiding readers to find their true potential and manifest their deepest desires.

A MEMORABLE FANCY (4)

Once, I saw a Devil in a flame of fire, who arose before an Angel that sat on a cloud, and the Devil uttered these words: "The worship of God is honoring His gifts in other men, each according to his genius, and loving the greatest men best. Those who envy or calumniate great men hate God, for there is no other God."

The Angel, hearing this, became almost blue, but mastering himself, he grew yellow, and at last white-pink and smiling, and then replied: "Thou idolater, is not God One? And is not He visible in

The Alchemy of Vision

Jesus Christ? and has not Jesus Christ given His sanction to the law of ten commandments? And are not all other men fools, sinners, and nothings?"

The Devil answered: "Bray a fool in a mortar with wheat, yet shall not his folly be beaten out of him. If Jesus Christ is the greatest man, you ought to love Him to the greatest degree. Now, hear how He has given His sanction to the law of the Ten Commandments. Did He not mock at the Sabbath, and so mock the Sabbath's God? murder those who were murdered because of Him? Turn away the law from the woman taken in adultery, steal the labor of others to support Him? Bear false witness when He omitted to make a defense before Pilate? Covet when He prayed for His disciples, and when He bid them shake off the dust of their feet against such as refused to lodge them? I tell you, no virtue can exist without breaking these ten commandments. Jesus was all virtue and acted from impulse, not from rules."

When he had so spoken, I beheld the Angel, who stretched out his arms embracing the flame of fire, and he was consumed and arose as Elijah.

Note.—This Angel, who is now become a Devil, is my particular friend; we often read the Bible together in its infernal or diabolical sense, which the world shall have if they behave well.

I also have the Bible of Hell, which the world shall have

whether they will or no. One law for the lion and ox is Oppression.

Introduction:

In this fourth Memorable fancy, we delve into a profound dialogue between a Devil and an Angel, as depicted by William Blake, exploring the themes of divinity, virtue, and the interpretation of religious law. Neville Goddard's philosophical lens offers a unique perspective on this conversation, highlighting the dynamic interplay between human perception, divine law, and the power of belief.

Context Setting:

Blake's narrative presents a fiery debate about God, virtue, and religious interpretation. The Devil, symbolizing a challenging voice, confronts traditional views represented by the Angel. Through this, Blake questions the nature of divinity and moral absolutes.

Analysis:

- The Devil's Argument: The Devil's provocative statement suggests that honoring the divine in others is the true worship of God. This aligns with Goddard's concept that God exists within each individual and that recognizing and valuing the divine in others is a form of honoring the universal God.

- The Angel's Response and Transformation: The Angel's

transition from a state of shock to acceptance and transformation into a Devil symbolizes the evolution of belief. This reflects Goddard's idea that beliefs are fluid and can transform our understanding of the divine.

- Questioning Religious Dogma: The Devil's critique of Jesus Christ and the Ten Commandments invites a reevaluation of traditional religious doctrines. Goddard, who emphasized personal experience and imagination in understanding the divine, would likely view this as an encouragement to seek personal interpretations of spiritual truths.

- The Nature of Virtue: The Devil's claim that no virtue can exist without breaking the Ten Commandments challenges conventional morality. In Goddard's view, this could be interpreted as the idea that true virtue arises from an authentic, personal connection with the divine rather than strict adherence to external laws.

- The Embrace and Transformation: The Angel's embrace of the flame and transformation into Elijah is significant. This mirrors Goddard's teaching that personal transformation comes through an embrace of inner truths and spiritual fires, leading to enlightenment.

The Note – A New Perspective:

Blake's note suggests a radical reinterpretation of traditional scriptures. This resonates with Goddard's belief in the symbolic and personal nature of biblical stories. The idea of a "Bible of Hell" proposes an alternative, perhaps more human-centered, understanding of divine law.

Conclusion:

This chapter presents a complex interplay of ideas, challenging traditional religious views and highlighting the evolution of belief. Through Goddard's perspective, we see these dialogues as a metaphor for the individual's journey in understanding and internalizing divine principles. The transformation of the Angel into Elijah, a prophet of change and awakening, encapsulates the journey of spiritual evolution that both Blake and Goddard advocate – a journey from rigid dogma to personal, imaginative engagement with the divine.

Chapter Two
Introduction to Neville Goddard's Core Teachings

<u>Part One: Laying the Foundation   from Mystic to Modern Guide</u>

Neville Goddard, a 20th-century philosopher and mystic, emerged as a distinctive voice in spiritual thought, bridging the gap between esoteric traditions and modern seekers. While many philosophers dissected the nature of reality from a distance, Goddard insisted on the immediacy and practicality of spiritual truths.

The Power of Imagination

Central to Goddard's teachings is the notion of Imagination. He professed that our imagination is not just a whimsical faculty of the mind   but a potent force capable of shaping our reality.

"Imagination," he often said, "is God." It's through this lens that he encouraged his followers to re-envision their lives and the world around them.

Conscious Creation:

Goddard believed that we are all creators, constantly shaping our realities through our beliefs, feelings, and assumptions. By adjusting these internal states and becoming conscious creators, we can intentionally direct the course of our lives, bringing our desires and dreams into tangible existence.

The Promise and The Law:

Goddard's teachings revolve around two core concepts: The Promise and The Law. The Law states that our external world is a direct reflection of our internal state. Everything we experience is a result of our beliefs and assumptions. The Promise, on the other hand, delves into the profound spiritual transformation each individual can undergo, moving towards a realization of our divine nature.

Real-life Resonance:

Goddard's philosophies are not mere abstract concepts but are grounded in everyday experiences. Throughout his lectures and writings, he provided countless anecdotes – both personal and from his followers – as testimonies to the transformative power of his teachings. As we proceed, we'll delve into real-life examples that showcase how Goddard's principles have been applied, offering readers practical insights for integrating these teachings into their own lives.

Conclusion:

Neville Goddard, with his emphasis on the practical application of spiritual truths, has left an indelible mark on countless seekers. His core teachings, though seemingly simple, contain profound depths that can transform one's perception of reality. As we journey through this chapter, we will unravel these teachings, grounding them in practical, everyday scenarios and exploring how they can serve as transformative tools for modern seekers.

Part Two: The Power of Imagination in Neville Goddard's Teachings

Introduction to the Immeasurable Imagination:

Neville Goddard's philosophy revolves around a single, powerful principle: the transformative capacity of the imagination. While many of us view imagination as a faculty reserved for artists or children, Goddard posits it as the very essence of our being, the divine spark within each individual.

Imagination as the Creative Force:

In the vast expanse of human faculties, imagination stands paramount in Goddard's teachings. He believed that everything we witness in the external world, from the tangible artifacts of human creation to the circumstances of our personal lives, originates from imaginative acts. This concept elevates imagination from mere daydreaming to the status of a divine tool wielded by each of us, often unconsciously.

The Realm of Assumptions and Belief:

Goddard often emphasized the significance of assumptions in shaping our reality. When we assume a certain outcome, feeling, or state, we're essentially imagining it into existence. Our deeply held beliefs and feelings germinate in the fertile ground of imagination, which then orchestrates the events and circumstances to bring them to fruition. For Goddard, recognizing and harnessing this process is crucial to intentional living.

Living in the End:

One of the core techniques Goddard taught his followers is the practice of "living in the end." Instead of hoping or wishing for a desired outcome, he encouraged individuals to inhabit the feeling of their wish fulfilled, to immerse themselves fully in the scenario where their dreams have already materialized. This imaginative act not only shifts one's internal state but also sets into motion the external manifestations that align with this new reality.

Bridging the Physical and the Metaphysical:

For Goddard, imagination serves as the bridge between our physical reality and the metaphysical realm of possibilities. By accessing and directing our imaginative faculties, we can tap into this reservoir of potential and reshape our world. The barriers that exist are not in the external world but within our own self-imposed limits. By expanding our imaginative capacities, we break free from these constraints.

Real-world Ramifications:

While Goddard's teachings may seem esoteric, their real-world applications are tangible. Consider an inventor envisioning a groundbreaking device or an athlete visualizing their victory before a pivotal match. These are not just acts of positive thinking but the conscious channeling of imaginative energy toward manifesting a specific reality.

Transformation Beyond Materialism:

Although many are drawn to Goddard's teachings for material manifestations – better jobs, relationships, or health – the true essence of his philosophy is transformational and transcendent. By recognizing our innate power and the divine nature of our imaginative faculty, individuals are empowered to rise above mere material desires and journey toward self-realization and spiritual enlightenment.

Conclusion:

In a world often ruled by externalities and seeming limitations, Goddard's teachings on the power of imagination emerge as a beacon of hope and empowerment. By recognizing and harnessing this divine faculty, individuals can not only shape their external circumstances but also embark on a profound inner journey of discovery and transformation. As we proceed, we will further explore how these teachings can be practically applied, offering readers tools and insights for a life of conscious creation and boundless potential.

Part Three: Alignment with Blake's Visionary Concepts

Introduction to a Shared Vision

In the pantheon of thinkers, Neville Goddard and William Blake might initially seem like figures from disparate backgrounds—one a mystic philosopher of the 20th century and the other a visionary poet and artist from the Romantic era. Yet, a closer look reveals striking parallels in their understanding of the human experience, imagination, and reality.

Imagination as the Divine Instrument

Both Blake and Goddard recognized the supreme power of imagination. For Blake, imagination was the eternal human essence, the force that transcends temporal and spatial confines, echoing through his artistic endeavors. Goddard, in his own way, championed imagination as the very tool that shapes our physical reality, insisting that through it, we co-create our world. Their shared perspective identifies imagination as both the divine spark within humanity and its most potent transformative tool.

The Realm Beyond Reason

Blake often expressed his skepticism toward the empiricist outlook, emphasizing a transcendent understanding that went beyond mere reason. Goddard echoed this sentiment, asserting that while reason and logic have their place, it's the imagination that truly guides our destiny, often beyond the confines of rationality. Both visionaries encourage stepping beyond the limiting scope of mere logical understanding to embrace a broader, more holistic perspective.

Contradictions and Unity

Just as Blake delved into the interplay of opposing forces in "The Marriage of Heaven and Hell," Goddard's teachings often allude to the balance of desires and fears, beliefs and doubts. Both suggest that in the embrace and understanding of these seeming contradictions, profound truths and transformations are realized.

The Visionary Experience

Blake's works are renowned for their visionary and prophetic undertones. Similarly, Goddard's teachings often delve into the idea of accessing future states in the present moment, "living in the end." Both figures share the perspective that time, as commonly understood, can be transcended through the imaginative and visionary experience.

Conscious Creation and Divine Humanity

In both Blake's and Goddard's philosophies, there's an intrinsic belief in the divine nature of humanity. Blake's assertion of mankind's inherent divinity resonates with Goddard's teachings that every individual, through their imaginative act, can tap into this divine power, manifesting their desires and shaping their reality.

Conclusion

The alignment of Neville Goddard's teachings with William Blake's visionary concepts underscores the timeless nature of their shared insights. Though separated by centuries, their ideas converge in a profound understanding of the human spirit, the power of imagination, and the boundless potential within each individual. As we venture deeper into the intertwining of these two philosophical giants, we'll further explore how their combined wisdom offers a roadmap for those seeking greater understanding, purpose, and transformative power in their lives.

Part Four: Practical Applications of Goddard's Teachings

Introduction to Actionable Wisdom

While Neville Goddard's teachings delve into profound realms of metaphysics and consciousness, their true magic lies in their practicality. His lessons are not mere philosophical musings but actionable guidelines that anyone can incorporate into daily life to manifest desires and shape reality. Below, we journey through some of these applications.

1. Living in The End

Concept: Imagine your life as if your desires have already been fulfilled. Feel the emotional and physical sensations associated with this realization.

Practical Application: If you seek a new job, instead of focusing on the process, envision yourself in your desired position. Feel the satisfaction, the environment, and even the handshake of your new employer. Make this visualization a daily practice.

2. The Power of Assumption

Concept: By assuming the feeling of the wish fulfilled, you align yourself with its manifestation.

Practical Application: Instead of wishing for good health, assume the feeling of being healthy. Adopt the posture, actions, and thoughts of a healthy individual. This assumption reinforces the desired state of health in your reality.

3. Mental Conversations

Concept: Your inner conversations shape your outer reality. Guard them, ensuring they are constructive and aligned with your desires. I can't stress enough how important it is to be mindful and recognize our internal conversations.

Practical Application: If you wish to mend a strained relationship, instead of dwelling on past disagreements, have mental conversations that reflect understanding, love, and reconciliation with the person involved.

4. Sleep Technique

Concept: As you drift into sleep, it's an opportune time to impress your subconscious with your desires.

Practical Application: Before sleeping, replay a scene in your mind that implies your wish has been fulfilled. This could be a congratulatory conversation or a moment of personal achievement. Let this scene loop until you fall asleep.

5. Revision Technique

Concept: Revisit and revise any negative or unwanted events of the day in your imagination to better align with your desires.

Practical Application: If you had a disagreement with a colleague, rather than replaying the disagreement in your mind, reimagine it. Visualize a productive conversation where both parties leave satisfied.

6. The Golden Rule Applied Imaginatively

Concept: Wish for others what you'd wish for yourself. By sending out positive intentions, you attract similar energies.

Practical Application: If you wish for prosperity, imagine your friends, family, and even strangers being prosperous. Feel genuine happiness for their success, knowing the universe mirrors this energy back to you.

7. Persistent Assumption

Concept: Regardless of external circumstances, persist in the assumption that your desire is fulfilled until it hardens into fact.

Practical Application: If you're aiming for a particular career milestone, don't be swayed by temporary setbacks. Remain steadfast in your assumption, focusing on the end goal rather than the obstacles.

Conclusion

Neville Goddard's teachings offer a treasure trove of tools for those willing to venture into the landscape of their imagination. By understanding and applying these practices, one doesn't merely grasp a philosophy; they equip themselves with a potent arsenal to transform the world from the inside out. As we delve deeper into these teachings, we'll uncover more layers of their transformative potential, bridging the gap between the ethereal and the tangible.

Part Five: The Transformative Power of Imagination and Consciousness

The realm of human imagination and consciousness is an enigma, both vast and intimate. While the power of the mind has been lauded across civilizations and eras, Neville Goddard pioneered a distinct exploration into the incredible potential it harnesses. At the heart of his teachings lies the belief that our internal landscapes shape our external realities, painting a vivid picture of life's infinite possibilities.

The Infinite Canvas of Imagination

Imagination, for Goddard, wasn't a mere child's play or a fleeting whimsy. It was the sculpting tool of reality. Every great invention, artistic masterpiece, or societal shift started as a mere thought, an image in someone's mind. This mental projection holds the seed of potentiality.

Leonardo da Vinci once visualized machines that could fly, and centuries later, we conquered the skies. Martin Luther King dreamt of equality, a vision that transformed societies. These luminaries accessed the realm of imagination, allowing their inner visions to chart the course of their external worlds.

Consciousness: The Observing Self

Consciousness, as Goddard elucidates, is more than

The Alchemy of Vision

awareness; it's the lens through which we interpret and interact with our realities. Our beliefs, feelings, and assumptions are the filters of this lens, coloring every experience. By understanding and adjusting these filters, we gain the prowess to shift our worlds.

Imagine two individuals witnessing a sunset. One, recently heartbroken, sees it as a melancholic end, while another, freshly in love, views it as a promise of beautiful tomorrows. The event is constant, but the interpretations stemming from their consciousness are worlds apart.

The Symphony of Imagination and Consciousness

When imagination and consciousness dance in harmony, a symphony of manifestation ensues. Goddard proposes that when we vividly imagine a scenario and root it in the consciousness of it being real, we align with its frequency, drawing it into our physical realm.

Consider an aspiring musician who imagines playing at a grand concert as this vision becomes a recurring occupant of his consciousness, his actions, decisions, and serendipities align, eventually leading him to that very stage.

Altering the Tapestry of Reality

Every individual, knowingly or unknowingly, weaves their reality tapestry daily. With every thought, feeling, and assumption, they're either reinforcing existing patterns or stitching new designs.

Goddard's teachings empower us to become conscious weavers, selecting threads of choice rather than settling for handed-down patterns.

A woman trapped in the cycle of financial scarcity can alter her reality by consistently imagining abundance, feeling its reality, and allowing her consciousness to dwell in this new state. Over time, opportunities and pathways she hadn't noticed before began to emerge.

The Pitfalls of Unconscious Creation

Not all creations stem from conscious intent. Many of our realities are products of passive acceptance or inherited beliefs. Goddard warns of the traps of unconscious creation, where we let external events or old scripts dictate our lives.

A man who grew up hearing about the hardships of life might unknowingly accept struggle as his destiny. This belief, even if unspoken, shapes his reality. But upon recognizing this passive creation, he can choose a different narrative, one of ease and prosperity.

Reality: A Reflective Mirror

The external world, in Goddard's perspective, is a reflective mirror, echoing our internal states. This isn't a metaphorical assertion but a literal one. If we harbor feelings of unworthiness, the world reflects scenarios confirming this belief. Conversely, if we radiate confidence and joy, our environments respond in kind.

It's akin to tuning a radio. When we adjust our internal frequencies (beliefs and feelings), the external stations (experiences) we receive shift accordingly.

Awakening to the God Within

Central to Goddard's teachings is the belief that every individual holds divine potential. We're not mere mortals navigating fate but gods sculpting destiny. By recognizing and harnessing the symbiotic powers of imagination and consciousness, we step into this divine role, orchestrating realities of our choosing.

This isn't about inflated egos or superiority complexes but a profound realization of our innate capabilities. As we awaken to this inner deity, limitations dissolve, replaced by boundless horizons.

Conclusion

Neville Goddard's deep dive into imagination and consciousness isn't merely philosophical musing; it's a clarion call to humanity. A call to recognize our inherent might, to shift from passive participants to active creators, to embrace the divine potential we all cradle. By understanding and integrating the transformative power of imagination and consciousness, we don't just change our realities; we redefine the very essence of life itself.

Chapter Three
Exploring the Union of Reason and Imagination

Part One: Neville Goddard's Interpretation of "The Marriage of Heaven and Hell"

The Marriage: More than Mere Conjoining

In Goddard's view, the marriage spoken of by Blake wasn't a mere juxtaposition of opposites but a profound unification, a synthesis. Blake's heaven and hell weren't realms of rewards and punishments but symbols representing reason and imagination, respectively.

Imagine a vast canvas where Heaven, the realm of structure, order, and predictability (reason), intersects with Hell, the realm of passion, chaos, and creativity (imagination). Their union, rather than resulting in conflict, forms a harmonious dance, creating a tapestry of infinite potentialities.

Reason: The Binding Framework

To Goddard, reason represents the skeletal structure of existence. It's the logic, the rationale, the foundational principles that govern our world. It's the container, the defined space within which the substance of life plays out.

The Alchemy of Vision

Consider the laws of physics. They dictate the behavior of the cosmos, from galaxies to atoms. They're unwavering and consistent, providing a stable framework. Without them, chaos would ensue, and existence, as we know it, wouldn't be.

Imagination: The Limitless Expanse

Contrasting reason's boundaries is imagination, the boundless expanse where anything is possible. Goddard revered imagination as the divine force, the creative essence that breathes life into the skeletal framework of reason.

Think of a blank piece of paper (reason) and an artist with a palette of endless colors (imagination). The paper sets the boundary, while the artist, unrestricted by the canvas's size, can create countless masterpieces.

Goddard's View: A Symphonic Interplay

Goddard believed that life, in its truest essence, is the symphonic interplay between reason and imagination. Neither can exist in isolation. Pure reason, devoid of imagination, becomes sterile, rigid, and lifeless. Conversely, unbridled imagination, without reason's framework, can lead to chaos and ungrounded fantasies.

Blake's Vision Through Goddard's Lens

While Blake's "The Marriage of Heaven and Hell" has been

subject to numerous interpretations, Goddard's lens offers a pragmatic approach. Blake's Proverbs of Hell, which seem paradoxical, align seamlessly with Goddard's philosophy. For instance, when Blake states, "What is now proved was once only imagined," he echoes Goddard's conviction about imagination's power to shape reality.

To Goddard, this wasn't a mere poetic flourish but an affirmation. Before any scientific discovery becomes a proven fact, it exists as an imaginative idea in someone's mind. The airplane, the internet, the vaccine—all once figments of imagination, now tangible realities.

The Practical Implication of This Marriage

Goddard's interpretation isn't purely philosophical; it's profoundly practical. By understanding the union of reason and imagination, we can shape our personal realities. Reason helps us discern, make choices, and navigate life's complexities. In tandem, imagination allows us to transcend perceived limitations, envisioning realities beyond present circumstances.

For someone trapped in a cycle of poverty, reason provides an understanding of their current situation, the choices leading there, and the practical steps needed for change. Imagination, on the other hand, offers a vision of abundance, a reality where their current circumstances are but a distant memory.

Conclusion

Through the interpretive genius of Neville Goddard, William Blake's "The Marriage of Heaven and Hell" gains renewed relevance for contemporary seekers. This union, symbolizing the dance of reason and imagination, isn't just an artistic concept but a practical blueprint. It's a guide on how to navigate the terrain of existence, leveraging the stability of reason and the transformative power of imagination, ultimately leading us towards a life of purpose, meaning, and infinite potentialities.

Part Two: The Profound Understanding of Spiritual Truth

The pursuit of spiritual truth is as ancient as humanity itself. Generations have sought to pierce the veil of material reality, to unearth the deeper, more profound truths that lie beneath the surface of our existence. Through the lens of Neville Goddard's teachings and building upon William Blake's visionary concepts, we embark on a journey to gain a more profound understanding of these spiritual truths.

Unraveling the Spiritual Fabric

Goddard believed that our physical world is but a reflection, a manifestation of a deeper spiritual reality. This realm isn't distant or separate; it's intricately woven into the very fabric of our existence. Every moment, every experience carries within it a spiritual truth waiting to be discovered.

Consider the beauty of a rose: its intricate petals, its intoxicating fragrance. While it provides sensory pleasure, at a deeper level, it stands as a testament to the marvels of creation, to the intricate balance and harmony of life.

The Truth of Imagination

Central to Goddard's teachings is the belief in the transformative power of imagination. For him, imagination wasn't mere daydreaming; it was the divine creative force. By harnessing this power, individuals could shape their realities, not just in a

The Alchemy of Vision

metaphorical sense but in tangible, real-world outcomes.

The story of the Wright brothers serves as a fitting example. The idea of human flight was once relegated to the realms of fantasy and mythology. Yet, through the power of sustained imagination and unyielding belief, what was once deemed impossible became a soaring reality.

Spiritual Truth in Everyday Life

Goddard's philosophy emphasizes the presence of spiritual truths in our daily lives. Every challenge, every joy, every sorrow carries within it a lesson, an insight into the deeper workings of the universe. By recognizing and understanding these truths, we can lead lives of greater purpose and meaning.

Consider the challenges of the past year. While they may have been fraught with difficulty, they also provided opportunities for growth, reflection, for a deeper understanding of oneself and the world around.

The Eternal Dance of Opposites

Drawing inspiration from Blake's "The Marriage of Heaven and Hell," Goddard delved into the interplay of opposites. Life and death, joy and sorrow, success and failure - these aren't disparate entities but part of an eternal dance, each giving meaning to the other. Recognizing this interplay is pivotal in grasping spiritual truths.

Think of the ebb and flow of the ocean tides. The high tide

is defined by the low and vice versa. This rhythmic dance, this perpetual cycle, mirrors the nature of our experiences.

The Ultimate Truth: The I AM

Perhaps the most profound spiritual truth in Goddard's teachings is the concept of "I AM." This isn't just an affirmation; it's an acknowledgment of one's divine nature, a recognition that the individual and the universal are intricately linked. By understanding and embodying this truth, one can transcend perceived limitations and step into a realm of infinite possibilities.

Every great spiritual teacher, from Christ to Buddha, echoed this truth in their teachings. "The kingdom of God is within you." "Look within, and you shall find." These aren't just poetic statements but profound truths, urging us towards self-realization.

Conclusion

The quest for spiritual truth is both an inward journey and an outward exploration. Through the teachings of Neville Goddard and the visionary concepts of William Blake, we gain invaluable insights, allowing us to navigate the complexities of existence with clarity, purpose, and profound understanding. As we delve deeper, we realize that these truths aren't esoteric concepts but living realities waiting to be embraced and embodied in every moment of our lives.

Chapter Four
Applying Neville Goddard's Principles to Personal Growth

<u>Part One: Unleashing the Creative Powers Within</u>

The journey of self-betterment is paved with countless methodologies, philosophies, and self-help doctrines. Yet, amidst this sea of resources, the teachings of Neville Goddard stand out as uniquely transformative. His principles, rooted in the power of imagination and conscious creation, can be invaluable tools for personal growth. Here, we'll dive deep into these principles and explore their practical application in our lives.

1. Understanding the Core Principles

The "I AM" Consciousness: Goddard's philosophy is anchored in the belief that imagination creates reality and that we can shape our world through our beliefs and assumptions. At the core is the "I AM" consciousness, the belief in oneself as the operant power and creator of one's reality.

Example: Consider someone who repeatedly thinks, "I am unlucky in love." This belief could manifest in reality, leading them to subconsciously sabotage potential relationships. By shifting this belief to "I AM deserving of love and happiness," they change their reality.

2. The Law of Assumption

According to Goddard, when you assume something as true, even without physical evidence, it becomes your reality. This is the foundation for manifesting desires.

Example: A woman aspiring to be a manager might start by assuming the role mentally, embodying the confidence and leadership qualities associated with it. Over time, her behavior might align with this mental image, leading her to actualize her aspirations.

3. The Feeling is the Secret

Goddard emphasizes that feeling the wish fulfilled is essential for manifestation. It's not enough to simply visualize; one must feel and believe that the desired outcome is already real.

Example: A student wishing to ace an exam shouldn't just visualize a high score but should also feel the joy, pride, and relief associated with that achievement.

4. Revision

Goddard believed in the power of revising an undesirable event in one's mind. By mentally reconstructing the event as you wish it had unfolded, you can shift your feelings and subsequent manifestations.

Example: After a disagreement with a friend, instead of

ruminating on the negative emotions, one can mentally "rewrite" the event, imagining a peaceful resolution. This helps in healing the emotional wound and might also pave the way for reconciliation.

5. Living in the End

This principle urges individuals to live as if their desires have already been realized. By embodying the final outcome, the universe aligns to make that vision a reality.

Example: Someone starting a business should not just dream of success but should operate and make decisions as if the business is already thriving.

6. Persistent Assumption

Manifestation requires persistence. Holding steadfastly to your desired outcome, even in the face of evidence to the contrary, reinforces your belief and accelerates the realization of your desires.

Example: An aspiring writer facing rejection should persistently assume success, continuing to write and submit work, driven by the unwavering belief in their inevitable success.

Conclusion

Neville Goddard's teachings provide a robust framework for personal growth. By understanding and applying these principles, we can harness the limitless power of our imagination and consciousness. Personal growth, then, becomes not a quest for external validation but an inward journey of realization and manifestation. As Goddard himself said, "Change your conception of yourself, and you will automatically change the world in which you live."

Part Two:
Practical Techniques for Enhancing Imagination and Consciousness

The power of imagination and heightened consciousness can profoundly transform our reality. However, nurturing and harnessing these faculties requires consistent practice and deliberate effort. Below are practical techniques, accompanied by real-life examples, that can help anyone amplify their imaginative and conscious capabilities.

1. Visualization Meditation

Technique: Dedicate a quiet moment each day to close your eyes and vividly imagine a desired outcome. Engage all your senses—what do you see, hear, feel, smell, and taste in this imagined reality?

Example: A young musician might visualize standing on a grand stage, feeling the weight of the guitar, and hearing the roar of the crowd.

2. Dream Journaling

Technique: Each morning, write down any dreams you recall. This practice not only boosts dream recall but also sharpens imaginative faculties.

Example: An artist might dream of a peculiar landscape. By

journaling and reflecting on it, they could discover new inspiration for their next artwork.

3. Affirmative Mantras

Technique: Create positive, present-tense statements that align with your desires. Repeat them aloud or in your mind daily.

Example: A person battling self-esteem issues might affirm, "I am worthy, I am loved, and I am confident." Over time, this can recalibrate their self-image.

4. Mindfulness and Presence

Technique: Practice grounding exercises, like focused breathing or noting sensory experiences, to cultivate presence. Being fully in the moment enhances consciousness.

Example: Someone feeling overwhelmed at work might take a five-minute break to focus solely on their breathing. This simple act can help center and rejuvenate them.

5. Engaging in Creative Outlets

Technique: Activities like painting, writing, or even gardening can stimulate the imagination and foster a deeper connection with one's inner self.

Example: A retired teacher takes up pottery and finds that shaping clay not only ignites her imagination but also fosters a deep sense of tranquility and connection.

6. Conscious Consumption of Art and Literature

Technique: Engage deeply with various art forms. When reading a book or viewing a painting, immerse yourself fully, pondering the underlying themes and emotions.

Example: A young writer immerses himself in classic literature, allowing vivid descriptions and intricate characters to expand his imaginative horizons.

7. Sensory Deprivation

Technique: Spend time in a sensory deprivation tank or simply lie in a dark, quiet room. By limiting external stimuli, the mind becomes more introspective.

Example: An entrepreneur facing burnout finds clarity and renewed creativity after a session in a sensory deprivation tank, emerging with fresh ideas for her business.

8. Engage in Conscious Conversations

Technique: Cultivate conversations that go beyond surface-level chatter. Discuss dreams, aspirations, and abstract concepts to expand consciousness.

Example: Two friends discussing the nature of time might find themselves exploring profound philosophical concepts, sharpening their cognitive faculties in the process.

Conclusion

Enhancing imagination and consciousness isn't a one-size-fits-all journey; it's deeply personal. Experiment with the techniques that resonate most and integrate them into daily life. With dedication, the transformational power of an awakened imagination and heightened consciousness can be within anyone's grasp.

Part Three:
Integrating Practices into Daily Life for Manifestation and Spiritual Growth

A deeper understanding of consciousness and imagination is only the beginning. For true transformation, these principles must be embedded into the fabric of daily life. Here's a roadmap to seamlessly integrate Neville Goddard's teachings and other enhancing practices into your everyday routine for tangible manifestation and spiritual ascent.

1. Morning Rituals

Technique: Start each day with intention. Develop a morning routine that includes practices like meditation, visualization, or affirmations. Set the tone for the day by consciously crafting your desired state.

Example: Lacy begins each day with a 10-minute meditation, visualizing her goals and reciting her affirmations. This sets a positive and purposeful tone for her day.

2. Mindful Moments

Technique: Carve out pockets of mindfulness throughout the day. Whether it's a five-minute breathing exercise or a moment of gratitude, these instances anchor you to the present.

Example: During his lunch break, Wesley steps outside,

taking a moment to feel the sun on his skin and express gratitude for the simple pleasures of life.

3. Evening Reflection

Technique: Dedicate time each evening to reflect on the day's events, emotions, and manifestations. This practice can help in recognizing patterns and adjusting intentions.

Example: Before bed, Calli journals about her day, noting any synchronicities or manifestations that occurred and adjusting her intentions for the following day.

4. Infuse Actions with Intent

Technique: Approach every action, no matter how small, with conscious intent. This aligns your energy with your desired outcomes.

Example: When preparing a meal, Allie infuses her cooking with love and intention, believing that the energy she puts into it will nourish both body and soul.

5. Create a Vision Board

Technique: A visual representation of your goals can serve as a daily reminder of your intentions and desires and help solidify them in your consciousness.

Example: Brayley creates a vision board filled with images of places she wants to visit, personal goals, and quotes that resonate with her. She places it in her workspace to constantly reinforce her intentions.

6. Continuous Learning

Technique: Dedicate time to study spiritual teachings, attend workshops, or join discussion groups. Continuously expand your understanding.

Example: Tillie attends a monthly book club where they discuss spiritual literature, deepening she grasp of manifestation and consciousness principles.

7. Embrace Challenges as Lessons

Technique: Instead of resisting setbacks, view them as opportunities for growth and spiritual refinement.

Example: When faced with a career setback, Mia reframes it as a chance to realign with her true passion, leading her to a more fulfilling professional path.

8. Cultivate a Supportive Community

Technique: Surround yourself with like-minded individuals who share similar spiritual and manifestation goals. This can create a powerful collective energy.

Example: Laura joins a manifestation circle, where members support each other's intentions, share experiences, and collectively amplify their manifestation powers.

Conclusion

True spiritual growth and successful manifestation aren't sporadic events; they are cultivated through consistent practice and conscious living. By integrating these practices into daily routines, one creates a life rich in intention, meaning, and profound transformation. Embrace this journey and witness the magic that unfolds.

Chapter 5:
Unveiling the Mysteries in Paradoxes

Introduction:

Paradoxes, by their very nature, challenge our logical frameworks. They seem contradictory yet convey profound truths that transcend linear thinking. Both Neville Goddard and William Blake, in their spiritual and poetic explorations, embraced the enigma of paradoxes, urging us to venture beyond the surface to unearth deeper spiritual insights.

1. The Power in Surrender:

Overview: Many spiritual teachings assert that by relinquishing control, we harness true power. This paradox underscores that sometimes, by letting go, we align with a greater force, allowing our desires to manifest.

Blake's Perspective: Blake often wrote about surrendering to divine will, hinting that through surrender, we find our true selves.

Goddard's Take: Goddard believed in the power of detachment after visualization, indicating that once you've felt your wish fulfilled, release it to the universe.

2. The Known Unknown:

Overview: There's knowledge in recognizing our ignorance.

Acknowledging what we don't know can lead to deeper wisdom.

Blake's Perspective: Blake revered innocence and experience, hinting at the idea that with knowledge comes the understanding of our own limitations.

Goddard's Take: Goddard emphasized the mystery of the subconscious mind, suggesting that our conscious mind can't fathom its depths, yet it holds immense power.

3. Freedom in Boundaries:

Overview: Constraints can sometimes lead to genuine freedom. Through discipline and structure, we can attain spiritual liberation.

Blake's Perspective: Blake's portrayal of innocence in contrast to experience hints at the freedom found within the confines of innocence.

Goddard's Take: Goddard taught about the discipline of the mind and the focused use of imagination, highlighting how structured thought can lead to freedom in manifestation.

4. Solitude in Unity:

Overview: Within our individual experiences, we discover the universality of emotions and thoughts, realizing we're part of a collective whole.

Blake's Perspective: Blake often alluded to individual

experiences as a reflection of universal truths, suggesting that personal revelations hold cosmic significance.

Goddard's Take: For Goddard, individual imagination was a facet of the divine imagination, underscoring the interconnectedness of personal and universal experiences.

5. Complexity in Simplicity:

Overview: Simple truths can encompass vast complexities, and within straightforward principles, we can find profound depths.

Blake's Perspective: Through his seemingly simple poems and art, Blake conveyed profound metaphysical insights, revealing the complexity hidden within.

Goddard's Take: Goddard's teachings, though straightforward in their approach to imagination, offer intricate layers of understanding about the nature of reality.

Conclusion:

Paradoxes beckon us to look deeper, to question, and to embrace the mysteries of life. By exploring these enigmatic truths through the lenses of Blake and Goddard, we are invited to transcend traditional boundaries of understanding and step into a realm where contradictions coalesce into profound wisdom. As we unveil these mysteries, we're drawn closer to the essence of our existence and the universe's grand design.

MYCHAEL T. RENN

Introduction to Proverbs

As I was walking among the fires of Hell, delighted with the enjoyments of Genius, which to Angels look like torment and insanity, I collected some of their proverbs, thinking that as the sayings used in a nation mark its character, so the proverbs of Hell show the nature of infernal wisdom better than any description of buildings or garments.

When I came home, on the abyss of the five senses, where a flat-sided steep frowns over the present world, I saw a mighty Devil folded in black clouds hovering on the sides of the rock; with corroding fires, he wrote the following sentence now perceived by the minds of men, and read by them on earth:

"How do you know but every bird

that cuts the airy way

Is an immense world of delight,

closed by your senses five?"

In this section, we invite you to join us on this intellectual odyssey, walking among the fires of Hell, delighting in the enjoyment of Genius. As we decipher each proverb, we endeavor to reveal the larger nature of the infernal wisdom and its profound implications for our perception of reality.

Prepare yourself to embark on a journey of discovery,

The Alchemy of Vision

challenge your senses and your perceptions, and find delight in the unexpected. As Blake himself implies, every bird that cuts the airy way could be an immense world of delight, closed by our senses five. But perhaps, by pondering these proverbs together, we might unlock some of these hidden worlds.

So, welcome, reader. Let us dare to see through not just our five senses but through the lens of the mind. Welcome to the paradoxical world of William Blake's 'Proverbs of Hell .'

A memorable fancy. A breakdown of the introduction to the Proverbs of Hell

"As I was walking among the fires of Hell, delighted with the enjoyments of Genius, which to Angels look like torment and insanity..."

Blake presents himself as a traveler in Hell, yet unlike traditional depictions, he finds delight rather than torment. Here, "Genius" probably refers to the creative spirit or intellectual power. Blake implies that the perspectives of Heaven (Angels) and Hell are distinct; what seems like 'torment and insanity' to Angels (representing traditional morality or religious orthodoxy) is perceived as a source of delight and inspiration in Hell (which stands for creativity, energy, and rebellion against orthodoxy).

"I collected some of their proverbs, thinking that as the sayings used in a nation mark its character, so the proverbs of Hell show

the nature of infernal wisdom better than any description of buildings or garments."

Blake collects the proverbs of Hell as a means to understand its inherent character, believing that these proverbs will provide insight into the unconventional wisdom it holds. Proverbs, in this context, are likely to be paradoxical or subversive of conventional wisdom.

"When I came home, on the abyss of the five senses, where a flat-sided steep frowns over the present world..."

This likely refers to his return to the physical or earthly world, the realm of the 'five senses.' The 'flat-sided steep' suggests a precipitous edge or boundary between the sensual world and some other realm. It 'frowns over the present world,' indicating a looming, possibly oppressive presence.

"I saw a mighty Devil folded in black clouds hovering on the sides of the rock; with corroding fires, he wrote the following sentence now perceived by the minds of men, and read by them on earth..."

Blake describes a vision of a mighty Devil who inscribes a message with 'corroding fires.' This fiery message is now perceived and read by men on earth, implying that the insights or wisdom derived from Hell (creative energy, rebellion against the status quo) have permeated human consciousness.

The Alchemy of Vision

"How do you know but every bird that cuts the airy way Is an immense world of delight, closed by your senses five?"

This proverb questions the limitations of human perception. It suggests that every bird flying through the air might be a vast world of delight, but people, limited to their five senses, are unable to perceive it. This challenges the conventional perception of reality and advocates for a broader, deeper understanding of existence beyond the physical senses.

In sum, Blake's work represents a radical reinterpretation of religious symbolism to argue for the power of creativity, the importance of questioning orthodox beliefs, and the potential for a person's perception to expand beyond its normal limits.

MYCHAEL T. RENN

Proverbs of Hell

1. In seed-time learn; in harvest teach; in winter enjoy.
2. Drive your cart and your   plow over the bones of the dead.
3. The road of excess leads to the palace of wisdom.
4. Prudence is a rich, ugly old maid courted by Incapacity.
5. He who desires   but acts not   breeds pestilence.
6. The cut worm forgives the   plow.
7. Dip him in the river, who loves water.
8. A fool sees not the same tree that a wise man sees.
9. He whose face gives no light shall never become a star.
10. Eternity is in love with the productions of time.
11. The busy bee has no time for sorrow.
12. The hours of folly are measured by the clock, but of wisdom, no clock can measure.
13. All wholesome food is caught without a net or a trap.
14. Bring out the number, weight, and measure in a year of dearth.
15. No bird soars too high if he soars with his own wings.
16. A dead body revenges, not injuries.
17. The most sublime act is to set another before you.
18. If the fool would persist in his folly, he would become wise.
19. Folly is the cloak of knavery.
20. Shame is Pride's cloak.
21. Prisons are built with stones of law and brothels with bricks

of religion.

22. The pride of the peacock is the glory of God.
23. The lust of the goat is the bounty of God.
24. The wrath of the lion is the wisdom of God.
25. The nakedness of a woman is the work of God.
26. Excess of sorrow laughs excess of joy weeps.
27. The roaring of lions, the howling of wolves, the raging of the stormy sea, and the destructive sword are portions of Eternity too great for the eye of man.
28. The fox condemns the trap, not himself.
29. Joys impregnate, sorrows bring forth.
30. Let man wear the fell of the lion, woman the fleece of the sheep.
31. The bird a nest, the spider a web, man friendship.
32. The selfish smiling fool and the sullen frowning fool shall be both thought wise that they may be a rod.
33. What is now proved was once only imagined.
34. The rat, the mouse, the fox, the rabbit watch the roots; the lion, the tiger, the horse, the elephant watch the fruits.
35. The cistern contains the fountain overflows.
36. One thought fills immensity.
37. Always be ready to speak your mind, and a base man will avoid you.
38. Everything possible to be believed is an image of truth.

39. The eagle never lost so much time as when he submitted to learn of the crow.
40. The fox provides for himself, but God provides for the lion.
41. Think in the morning, act in the noon, eat in the evening, sleep in the night.
42. He who has suffered you to impose on him knows you.
43. As the plow follows words, so God rewards prayers.
44. The tigers of wrath are wiser than the horses of instruction.
45. Expect poison from the standing water.
46. You never know what is enough unless you know what is more than enough.
47. Listen to the fool's reproach; it is a kingly title.
48. The eyes of fire, the nostrils of air, the mouth of water, the beard of earth.
49. The weak in courage is strong in cunning.
50. The apple tree never asks the beech how he shall grow, nor the lion the horse how he shall take his prey.
51. The thankful receiver bears a plentiful harvest.
52. If others had not been foolish, we should have been so.
53. The soul of sweet delight can never be defiled.
54. When thou seest an eagle, thou seest a portion of Genius. Lift up thy head!
55. As the caterpillar chooses the fairest leaves to lay her eggs on, so the priest lays his curse on the fairest joys.

The Alchemy of Vision

56. To create a little flower is the labour of ages.
57. Damn braces; bless relaxes.
58. The best wine is the oldest, the best water the newest.
59. Prayers plough not; praises reap not; joys laugh not; sorrows weep not.
60. The head Sublime, the heart Pathos, the genitals Beauty, the hands and feet Proportion.
61. As the air to a bird or the sea to a fish, so is contempt to the contemptible.
62. The crow wished everything was black; the owl that everything was white.
63. Exuberance is Beauty.
64. If the lion was advised by the fox, he would be cunning.
65. Improvement makes straight roads, but the crooked roads without Improvement are roads of Genius.
66. Sooner murder an infant in its cradle than nurse unacted desires.
67. Where man is not, nature is barren.
68. Truth can never be told so as to be understood and not to be believed.
69. Enough! or Too much.

Proverb 1: "In seedtime learn, in harvest teach, in winter enjoy."

Analysis: This proverb encapsulates the rhythm of life, emphasizing the importance of adapting to and making the most of each season we encounter.

Interpretation:

- Stages of Growth: Each season in the proverb denotes a phase of our life journey. "Seedtime" represents moments of acquiring knowledge, "harvest" stands for sharing and imparting that wisdom, and "winter" symbolizes times of reflection and savoring achievements.

- Flow of Life: The proverb encourages individuals to move gracefully with life's flow, understanding that every phase has its unique beauty and purpose.

- Living in the Moment: Implicitly, this wisdom asks readers to be present in the current phase of their life, embracing its lessons and opportunities rather than constantly yearning for the next.

Neville Goddard's Perspective:

- Imagination as Seed: Goddard might interpret "seedtime" as the period when we plant our desires and beliefs in the fertile ground of our imagination. This is a stage of incubation and

The Alchemy of Vision

nurturing dreams.

- Manifestation and Sharing: "Harvest" could be viewed as seeing our imaginative seeds come to fruition, realizing our desires, and understanding the potential of our inner beliefs—making it the perfect time to share this knowledge.

- Reflection and Joy: With "winter," Goddard would likely emphasize the pleasure of recognizing how our inner beliefs shape our external realities and the importance of relishing the manifestations of our imaginative efforts.

Application to Everyday Life:

- Recognizing Life's Phase: Taking stock of where you are in life can offer clarity. Are you in a phase of gathering knowledge, imparting wisdom, or enjoying the outcomes? Recognizing this can guide your actions and mindset.

- Embrace the Now: Each season of life offers its lessons and joys. Instead of waiting for 'better times,' find value in the current moment.

Proverb 2: "Drive your cart and your plow over the bones of the dead."

Analysis:

This enigmatic proverb encourages breaking free from traditional norms and conventions, emphasizing the significance of forging one's unique path, even if it means moving beyond established beliefs or dogmas.

The Alchemy of Vision

Interpretation:

- Redefining Boundaries: The "cart" and "plow" symbolize tools of progress and cultivation. Driving them "over the bones of the dead" connotes breaking ground on territories traditionally seen as sacred or taboo.

- Challenging Tradition: At its core, this proverb speaks to the courage required to question and move past outdated conventions. The "bones of the dead" can represent old ideas, dogmas, or societal norms that might hold one back.

- Empowerment and Autonomy: This is a call for self-reliance, urging individuals to take control of their destiny, even if it means disrupting the status quo.

Neville Goddard's Perspective:

- Limitless Imagination: Goddard's teachings revolve around the limitless power of imagination and belief. In this proverb's context, he would likely emphasize the need to shun limiting beliefs, many of which are passed down through generations or societies.

- Manifesting Beyond Limitations: For Goddard, the act of driving over the bones signifies boldly manifesting one's desires without being restricted by past constraints or beliefs.

Application to Everyday Life:

- Questioning Norms: Encourage introspection. Are there old beliefs or societal expectations holding you back? This proverb prompts a reevaluation of such constraints.

- Bravery in Choices: In personal and professional choices, there might be moments that call for breaking away from tradition or convention. Remember, forging your own path can lead to unexpected and rewarding destinations.

Proverb 3: "The road of excess leads to the palace of wisdom."

Analysis:

This provocative proverb suggests that sometimes pushing boundaries, even to points of excess, can be a path to gaining profound insights and understanding.

Interpretation:

- Pushing Boundaries: The "road of excess" signifies going beyond societal norms or our own personal limits. By exploring these outer realms, we potentially learn more about ourselves and the world.

- Wisdom Through Experience: Wisdom isn't just gained from moderation or restraint but can also be learned through overindulgence and its consequences.

The Alchemy of Vision

- Duality of Experience: Implicit in this saying is the understanding that there's wisdom in both excess and moderation. Each has its lessons to teach.

Neville Goddard's Perspective:

- Experiencing to Manifest: Goddard might interpret the "road of excess" as fully immersing oneself in a desired state, feeling it in its entirety, even excessively so, to manifest it.

- Depth of Belief: The proverb aligns with Goddard's teachings that one has to genuinely believe and immerse themselves in their desires. By going to these depths, even if perceived as excess, one can tap into a deeper understanding or "wisdom" of their true power.

- Understanding Dualities: Goddard often stressed the interplay between the external world and internal beliefs. The "palace of wisdom" could be a realization of this duality through experiences of excess.

Application to Everyday Life:

- Growth Through Challenges: Don't shy away from experiences just because they challenge your boundaries. Sometimes, growth and understanding come from navigating the aftermath of our choices, even the excessive ones.

- Learn from Every Experience: Whether it's a time of restraint or indulgence, every moment offers a lesson. Be open to gaining wisdom from all of life's pathways.

Proverb 4: "Prudence is a rich, ugly old maid courted by incapacity."

Analysis:

This aphorism offers a nuanced critique of extreme caution. It portrays prudence not just as a virtue but when taken to the extreme, as an unattractive trait that only those incapable would gravitate toward.

Interpretation:

- Caution's Double-Edged Sword: While prudence generally stands for wise caution, this proverb paints it in a less favorable light. Taken to the extreme, being overly cautious may prevent one from truly living or taking necessary risks.

- The Suitors of Prudence: "Courted by incapacity" suggests that only those who are ineffective or lack the ability to act decisively value extreme caution. Essentially, incapacity finds solace in prudence because it provides an excuse for inaction.

- Beauty Beyond Surface-Level: The use of "ugly" isn't

necessarily physical but suggests that there's a lack of allure or passion in extreme caution. Life's beauty often requires risk.

Neville Goddard's Perspective:

- Active Imagination: Goddard preached about the power of the active imagination and decisively acting on one's beliefs. This proverb might resonate with his idea that being overly cautious can stymie one's imaginative potential.

- Inaction vs. Manifestation: Goddard would probably caution against letting prudence turn into indecision or inaction. For our desires to manifest, one must move beyond mere caution and take deliberate, passionate steps.

- Limiting Beliefs: Over-prudence can be seen as a manifestation of limiting beliefs, which Goddard believed hindered our true potential.

Application to Everyday Life:

- Balanced Decision-Making: While it's essential to be cautious, don't let excessive prudence hinder your progress. Embrace opportunities and take calculated risks when needed.

- Challenge Comfort Zones: If you find yourself hesitating

often, challenge yourself to step outside your comfort zone. Growth often lies beyond the realms of extreme caution.

Proverb 5: "He who desires but acts not breeds pestilence."

Analysis:

This proverb emphasizes the consequences of inaction. When one harbors desires but fails to pursue them, it leads to internal decay or negative outcomes, likened here to 'pestilence .'

Interpretation:

- Desire vs. Action: Having desires is natural, but not acting on them leads to stagnation. The proverb warns against the dangers of suppressed desires and dreams.

- Internal Turmoil: "Breeds pestilence" is a vivid metaphor suggesting that inactive desires can cultivate resentment, regret, or even self-destruction over time.

- The Power of Pursuit: The proverb encourages not just dreaming but also acting upon those dreams, emphasizing the importance of turning aspirations into actions.

Neville Goddard's Perspective:

- Desire's Role in Creation: Goddard believed that desires were divinely planted seeds meant to be manifested. Not acting upon these desires goes against the natural law of creation.

The Alchemy of Vision

- Manifestation through Action: While Goddard focused heavily on the imaginative act, he also believed in the physical act's role in manifestation. To him, not acting on one's desires would be a neglect of one's divine role in the creative process.

- Emotional Consequences: Just as the proverb mentions "pestilence," Goddard might suggest that failing to act on one's desires could lead to emotional and spiritual ailments.

Application to Everyday Life:

- Embrace Passion: If you're passionate about something, take steps, even small ones, to realize that dream or desire.

- Avoid Regret: To prevent future regrets, act on your current desires. Even if it doesn't lead to success, the journey itself will be rewarding.

- Seek Clarity: If you're unsure about a desire, seek clarity rather than suppressing it. Understand its origin and decide if it aligns with your life's direction.

Proverb 6: "The cut worm forgives the plow."

Analysis:

This proverb touches on the theme of acceptance and resilience in the face of adversity or transformation. Even if the worm is harmed by the plow, it does not harbor resentment, implying a sense of acceptance or even gratitude for the larger process at play.

Interpretation:

- Nature's Resilience: The worm, despite facing harm, continues its existence without holding grudges. It represents nature's tenacity and ability to adapt and move forward.

- Greater Good: The plow may harm the worm, but it is essential for tilling the soil and fostering growth. This can be seen as recognizing the broader picture or accepting momentary setbacks for a more significant purpose.

- Acceptance: Holding onto resentment can be more damaging than the initial harm. The proverb highlights the importance of forgiveness and acceptance in healing and progression.

Neville Goddard's Perspective:

- Greater Plan: Goddard might suggest that everything, including adversities, plays a role in the grand scheme of our imaginative acts and manifestations. Sometimes, obstacles or setbacks serve a larger purpose in our journey.

- Power of Acceptance: Holding onto negative feelings or

The Alchemy of Vision

resentments can hinder our manifestations. Accepting, forgiving, and moving forward allows us to remain aligned with our desired end.

- Transformation Through Adversity: Just as the soil benefits from the plow's work despite the cutworm's harm, individuals can grow and transform through challenges if they approach them with the right mindset.

Application to Everyday Life:

- Embrace Challenges: Instead of resisting adversity, consider what it might be teaching you or how it fits into a bigger picture in your life.

- Let Go of Resentment: Holding onto negative feelings can be a roadblock to personal growth. Practice forgiveness, both for others and for yourself.

- Trust the Process: Even if you can't see it now, believe that every experience is shaping you for a greater purpose or end.

Proverb 7: "Dip him in the River who loves water."

Analysis:

This paradoxical saying encourages direct experience as the most authentic way of understanding and highlights the consequences of one's professed desires or beliefs, especially when they go against mainstream conventions or dogmas.

Interpretation:

- Direct Experience: Professing a love or belief in something is different from experiencing it firsthand. To truly understand or appreciate something, one must immerse oneself in it fully.

- Challenge of Convictions: Loving water and being submerged in it are two distinct experiences. This might allude to the idea of questioning if one's beliefs can stand the test of true experience or scrutiny.

- Irony and Authenticity: The proverb exudes a certain irony, pushing individuals to reflect on the authenticity of their proclaimed beliefs, especially when they align merely with societal or religious expectations.

Neville Goddard's Perspective:

- Living in the End: Goddard speaks about "living in the end," which involves feeling and acting as if your desires are already fulfilled. Similarly, if one claims to love or believe in something, they should be ready to experience it fully.

- Authentic Desire: Only by immersing oneself in the actual experience can we validate our true desires and beliefs, separating mere words from genuine feelings.

Application to Everyday Life:

- Challenge Your Beliefs: Before advocating for a belief or desire, subject it to the test of direct experience. This will ensure your convictions are based on genuine understanding rather than mere parroting of societal views.

- Seek Authenticity: In a world filled with echo chambers, ensure your beliefs and passions are genuinely your own. Dive deep into your interests, ensuring they're rooted in personal experience and not just surface-level affirmations.

- Embrace Consequences: If you truly stand by a belief, be ready to face the consequences, be they positive or challenging, of that conviction.

Proverb 8: "A fool sees not the same tree that a wise man sees."

Analysis:

This proverb delves into the subjectivity of perception, suggesting that wisdom dramatically alters how one perceives the world. What might seem ordinary or inconsequential to some may hold profound significance to those with deeper insight or understanding.

Interpretation:

- Subjectivity of Perception: Reality is not an objective

constant; it's shaped and molded by our experiences, knowledge, and wisdom. Two people can look at the same thing and perceive it entirely differently.

- Depth of Understanding: A wise individual tends to see beyond the surface, discerning deeper meanings, connections, and truths that might elude others.

- Challenging Surface Reality: Just as Blake often confronted conventional religious views and societal norms, this proverb encourages questioning surface interpretations and seeking a deeper understanding.

Neville Goddard's Perspective:

- Reality Molded by Beliefs: Goddard posited that our external world is shaped by our internal beliefs. Thus, a wise man, aware of his imaginative and creative power, would perceive the tree (or any reality) differently, influenced by his conscious beliefs and intentions.

- Inner Vision: Just as the wise man sees the tree differently, individuals can train their inner vision to perceive the world in a way that aligns with their desires and beliefs, thus influencing their external reality.

The Alchemy of Vision

Application to Everyday Life:

- Seek Depth: Don't just accept things at face value. Dive deeper, ask questions, and strive for a richer understanding of the world around you.

- Challenge Your Perception: Recognize that your current view of the world is not absolute. It's shaped by myriad factors, and with wisdom and experience, it can change and evolve.

- Wisdom Through Experience: Accumulate experiences, learn from them, and always be open to altering your perception based on newfound knowledge.

Proverb 9: "He whose face gives no light shall never become a star."

Analysis:

This proverb emphasizes the importance of inner radiance and authenticity. It suggests that those who do not emit inner brilliance or truth cannot expect to shine brightly or be recognized in the vast expanse of existence.

Interpretation:

- Inner Radiance: The "light" mentioned in the proverb refers to qualities like wisdom, authenticity, and genuine passion.

It's not merely about external appearances but about the inherent glow that comes from a well-lived, introspective life.

- Recognition & Influence: Much like stars that shine brightly in the night sky and guide travelers, individuals who exude genuine qualities are more likely to stand out and influence others.

- Confronting Superficiality: In a Blakean spirit of challenging societal norms, this proverb critiques the shallow pursuit of fame without substance and the transient nature of such fame.

Neville Goddard's Perspective:

- Emanation of Belief: Goddard would likely interpret the "light" as the external manifestation of one's firm beliefs and inner convictions. An individual who is deeply aligned with their beliefs and desires would naturally shine brighter.

- The Inner Creates the Outer: For Goddard, the internal state of being is reflected in the external world. Therefore, if one's inner state lacks light (conviction, belief, passion), it would be reflected in their external circumstances.

Application to Everyday Life:

- Cultivate Authenticity: Instead of chasing superficial recognition, focus on cultivating genuine qualities and knowledge. The recognition that comes from authenticity is more enduring and influential.

- Be True to Yourself: Embrace your unique qualities and let them shine. Do not dim your light to fit into societal molds.

- Seek Growth: Continuously strive for personal growth and enlightenment. It is through this growth that one's "face" truly begins to emit light.

Proverb 10: "Eternity is in love with the production of time."

Analysis:

At its heart, this proverb speaks to the relationship between the eternal and the transient. It suggests that while eternity is boundless and timeless, there's a fascination or love affair with the tangible, ever-changing nature of time.

The Alchemy of Vision

Interpretation:

- Interplay of Infinite and Finite: This proverb touches on the idea that eternity (the infinite) finds beauty or purpose in the finite realm of time. It's a poetic way to say that every fleeting moment is precious in the vast continuum of eternity.

- Sacredness of Moments: In the grand scope of eternity, each moment—no matter how brief—has significance. It's a reminder to cherish the now.

- Challenging Temporal Views: Blake often questioned societal and religious norms. This proverb may encourage us to look beyond traditional notions of time, suggesting that perhaps what we see as "temporary" has eternal significance.

Neville Goddard's Perspective:

- Manifestation in the Physical: Goddard believed that our imagination shapes reality. In this light, eternity (or the realm of infinite possibilities) cherishes the opportunity to manifest desires in the tangible world of time.

- Value in Experience: The process of desires coming to fruition, of dreams taking shape in the temporal world, might be what eternity values—an ever-unfolding dance between the potential and the actual.

Application to Everyday Life:

- Cherish Each Moment: Recognize the intrinsic value of every experience, knowing that in the vastness of eternity, each moment is a unique production.

- Manifest with Intention: Understand that you have the power to shape your reality. As you manifest your desires, you're playing a part in the grand play of eternity, expressing itself through time.

- Seek Depth: Look beyond the surface of fleeting experiences, seeking the eternal significance or lesson in each one.

Proverb 11: "The busy bee has no time for sorrow."

Analysis:

This proverb employs the metaphor of the industrious bee to underscore the concept of dedication, purpose, and the potential of focus to rise above adversity or melancholy.

Interpretation:

- Symbolism of the Busy Bee: The bee epitomizes hard work, diligence, and commitment. Bees are unwavering in their task of collecting nectar and creating honey, highlighting the virtues of purpose and dedication.

- Engrossment as Distraction: Being wholly absorbed in meaningful pursuits can act as a diversion from negative emotions, implying that passion can be an antidote to sorrow.

- Against Passive Despondency: In contrast to societal norms that might advocate for wallowing or remaining passive in the face of sorrow, this proverb suggests an active engagement in purposeful endeavors as a countermeasure.

Neville Goddard's Perspective:

- Purposeful Imagination: Goddard emphasized the power of the imagination to shape reality. Much like the bee, if one is wholly focused on their imaginative acts, they harness the power to transform their circumstances and emotions.

- Overcoming through Creation: Engaging the imagination and being involved in the act of conscious creation can act as a remedy for despair, just as the bee's industriousness keeps sorrow at bay.

Application to Everyday Life:

- Stay Engaged: Find something you're passionate about and immerse yourself in it. This not only provides a sense of purpose but can be therapeutic, offering solace during trying times.

- Reframe Perspective: When faced with challenges or sorrow, consider them as temporary and focus on tasks or goals that bring joy and meaning.

- Active Engagement: Rather than succumbing to feelings of despair seek out activities or pursuits that provide a sense of accomplishment and happiness, mirroring the bee's unwavering commitment to its tasks.

Proverb 12: "The hours of folly are measured by the clock, but of wisdom no clock can measure."

Analysis:

This saying delves into the contrasting natures of transient moments of foolishness and the eternal essence of wisdom. It comments on the temporal versus the timeless.

Interpretation:

- Temporal Folly vs. Timeless Wisdom: The proverb suggests that mistakes, missteps, or "folly" have a finite duration bound by the constraints of time. However, wisdom, once attained, is boundless and immeasurable.

- Beyond Physical Constraints: The folly is connected to the physical world, whereas wisdom transcends it. This highlights the ephemeral nature of our mistakes compared to the lasting impact of understanding.

- Rejecting Societal Metrics: By emphasizing that wisdom cannot be measured by any conventional means, the proverb challenges societal norms that often prioritize measurable achievements over intangible growth.

Neville Goddard's Perspective:

- Eternal Consciousness: Goddard would likely view this through the lens of our eternal consciousness and the idea that our true selves aren't confined by the limits of time and space. Mistakes (folly) are temporary and of this world, but wisdom speaks to the eternal nature of our beings.

- Depth of Understanding: To Goddard, understanding and embodying the power of imagination and consciousness would be the epitome of wisdom. Such profound insights are not transient but eternal.

Application to Everyday Life:

- Forgiving Folly: Understand that mistakes and errors are transient. They will pass and are merely momentary lapses, not defining traits.

- Valuing Growth: Prioritize learning and personal growth. While society might celebrate short-lived achievements, it's the enduring wisdom and understanding that truly enrich one's life.

- Timeless Wisdom: Recognize that true wisdom isn't about accumulating information but about deep understanding and insight, which is not bound by the confines of time.

Proverb 13: "All wholesome food is caught without a net or trap."

Analysis:

This adage delves into the purity of obtaining sustenance without manipulation or force. It speaks to the natural, unforced acquisition of what nourishes us, whether it be food, knowledge, or experiences.

Interpretation:

- Natural Acquisition: The proverb implies that the purest and most wholesome things in life are those that come to us naturally, without the need for contraptions or manipulation.

- Against Force and Manipulation: Using "net" and "trap" symbolically, Blake critiques society's tendencies to seize, control, or manipulate things, suggesting that the best things in life come without these efforts.

- Purity of Intent: At a deeper level, this could be a commentary on genuine intentions and interactions, suggesting that what's gained without deceit or cunning has a higher value.

Neville Goddard's Perspective:

- Natural Manifestation: Goddard's teachings emphasize the power of imagination in manifesting our desires. He would likely interpret this as suggesting that when one is in alignment with their true desires and imagines with clarity and intent, the desired outcomes will manifest naturally, without the need for force or manipulation.

- Flow of Consciousness: To Goddard, trying to force outcomes (using a "net or trap") is counterproductive. Instead, one should focus on cultivating a clear and positive consciousness, allowing manifestations to occur organically.

Application to Everyday Life:

- Genuine Relationships: In interpersonal interactions, it's the relationships formed without ulterior motives or manipulations that are the most genuine and fulfilling.

- Unforced Outcomes: In pursuits, whether personal or professional, allow outcomes to unfold naturally rather than trying to force or manipulate situations.

- Value Authenticity: Embrace authentic experiences,

relationships, and acquisitions, recognizing their inherent value over contrived or manipulated ones.

Proverb 14: "Bring out the number, weight, and measure in a year of dearth."

Analysis:

This saying touches on the significance of assessment, precision, and resourcefulness during challenging times. It underscores the importance of valuing and accounting for what one has when resources are scarce.

Interpretation:

- Resourcefulness in Hard Times: "A year of dearth" symbolizes a period of scarcity or difficulty. The proverb implies that in challenging times, it is essential to precisely know and evaluate what you have at your disposal.

- Valuation and Appreciation: By referencing "number, weight, and measure," Blake highlights the need to not only account for but also value and appreciate every resource, no matter how small or insignificant it might seem.

- Against Wastefulness: Implicitly, the proverb warns against frivolity and wastefulness, especially when resources are limited.

The Alchemy of Vision

Neville Goddard's Perspective:

- Conscious Appreciation: Goddard would likely infer that recognizing and valuing our present resources (both tangible and intangible, like our imagination) can help manifest abundance. During periods of lack, one should be more consciously appreciative and make the best use of what they have.

- Mindful Manifestation: Goddard might also view this proverb as a call to be more precise in one's imaginative acts, especially during challenging times, ensuring clarity in what one wants to manifest.

Application to Everyday Life:

- Mindful Consumption: In an age of consumerism, it's essential to evaluate and value what we already possess, understanding the worth of each item or experience.

- Optimizing Resources: Whether it's time, money, or energy, assess how you're using your resources, especially when they feel scarce. Make decisions that maximize their utility.

- Gratitude in Scarcity: During challenging times, cultivate a mindset of gratitude. Recognize and be thankful for what you have, making the most of it.

Proverb 15: "No bird soars too high if he soars with his own wings."

Analysis:

This proverb speaks to the power of individualism, self-reliance, and authenticity. It's a reminder that genuine achievements come when one relies on their unique abilities and not on borrowed strengths or external crutches.

Interpretation:

- Authenticity and Self-reliance: The bird symbolizes an individual, and its wings represent personal strengths, talents, and capabilities. To soar with one's wings implies achieving success by relying on one's innate abilities.

- Against Imitation: The proverb subtly warns against mimicking others or relying too heavily on external support. Achievements gained this way may lead one to fly too high, risking a great fall.

- Embracing One's Unique Path: Every individual has their unique trajectory, and this proverb encourages embracing and trusting that path, however high it might lead.

Neville Goddard's Perspective:

- Intrinsic Power of Imagination: Goddard would likely stress the inherent power of our imagination. Just as the bird relies on its wings, individuals should trust in their imaginative faculties to manifest their desires.

- Authentic Desires: Achievements and manifestations that are most fulfilling stem from desires that are genuinely our own, not those imposed or borrowed from societal expectations or others.

Application to Everyday Life:

- Trust Your Abilities: In a world that often promotes comparison, it's essential to believe in your skills, talents, and instincts. Trust that your unique capabilities are sufficient to achieve your dreams.

- Avoid Comparison: Don't measure your success by comparing it to others. Everyone has their path, and what works for one may not work for another. Celebrate your unique journey and accomplishments.

- Cherish Authenticity: Embrace and value authenticity, both in yourself and others. Recognize that genuine successes and joys come from staying true to oneself.

<u>Proverb 16: "A dead body revenges, not injuries."</u>

Analysis:

This proverb addresses the futility of holding onto grievances, highlighting the impermanence of life and the inevitability of death. It's a poignant reminder that, in the end, grudges and the desire for revenge are inconsequential.

The Alchemy of Vision

Interpretation:

- Futility of Revenge: A dead body cannot act, implying that revenge is a transient, fleeting desire that holds no weight in the grand scheme of life and death.

- Transient Nature of Life: The proverb suggests that, given the impermanence of life, it's futile to hold onto negative emotions or grudges.

- Rejection of Societal Vengefulness: At a deeper level, it can be viewed as a criticism of societal values that glorify revenge and retribution, urging individuals to rise above such impulses.

Neville Goddard's Perspective:

- Rise Above Negativity: Goddard emphasizes the power of positive imagination and feelings. This proverb aligns with his teachings, suggesting that it's more productive to focus on positive manifestations rather than dwell on negative emotions.

- Inner Transformation: Instead of seeking external revenge, one should aim for inner transformation and understanding, reshaping their reality with a more constructive mindset.

Application to Everyday Life:

- Let Go of Grudges: Understand the temporariness of life and the insignificance of holding onto negative emotions. Letting go can lead to a more fulfilling and peaceful existence.

- Embrace Forgiveness: Instead of seeking revenge, embrace forgiveness. It not only liberates the person you forgive but also frees you from the shackles of negativity.

- Seek Constructive Outlets: Channel your energy into positive endeavors. When faced with injuries or wrongdoings, look for constructive ways to cope, grow, and move forward.

Proverb 17: "The most sublime act is to set another before you."

Analysis:

This proverb emphasizes the noble nature of selflessness and prioritizing others over oneself. It showcases the idea that true greatness is found in acts of genuine altruism and kindness.

Interpretation:

- Virtue of Selflessness: The proverb heralds the virtue of placing someone else's needs or well-being above one's own, marking it as the highest form of human behavior.

The Alchemy of Vision

- Challenge to Egoistic Tendencies: It indirectly critiques individualistic or self-centered behavior, highlighting the richer, more fulfilling path of altruism.

- Rejection of Societal Self-Centeredness: It can also be viewed as a rebuke to societal norms that increasingly prioritize individual success and self-aggrandizement over communal well-being.

Neville Goddard's Perspective:

- Power of Positive Assumptions: By believing and assuming the best for another person, we align ourselves with the manifestation of positivity in both their life and ours.

- Generosity of Spirit: Goddard would likely concur that in the act of selflessly imagining good for another, we also elevate our own spirit and align with our desires.

Application to Everyday Life:

- Acts of Kindness: Small gestures of selflessness, like helping a neighbor or putting someone else's needs before yours, can profoundly impact your well-being and the world around you.

- Shift in Perspective: Instead of always prioritizing personal desires, try occasionally viewing situations from another's standpoint. This shift can lead to more harmonious relationships and personal growth.

- Empathetic Living: Embrace empathy. Actively trying to understand and feel for others enriches one's life experiences.

<u>Proverb 18: "If the fool would persist in his folly, he would become wise."</u>

Analysis:

This proverb suggests that mistakes and missteps, when pursued with consistency or reflected upon, can eventually lead to wisdom. It challenges the traditional notion that folly is inherently negative, instead positioning it as a potential pathway to deeper understanding.

Interpretation:

- Persistence Through Mistakes: Even if one starts on a path of folly, consistently pursuing it and learning from each mistake can ultimately lead to wisdom.

- Learning Curve: The proverb underscores that wisdom often comes from experience, even if those experiences initially seem foolish.

- Rejection of Quick Judgments: It critiques the societal

tendency to quickly label actions as wise or foolish, suggesting that true understanding requires a longer perspective.

Neville Goddard's Perspective:

- Persistent Imagining: Goddard might interpret "folly" as the persistent act of imagining a desired reality, even when it seems foolish or unlikely. By persisting in this "folly," one eventually aligns with their desired state.

- Growth from Experience: He would likely agree that personal growth and deeper understanding often arise from persistent experiences, even if they initially seem misguided.

Application to Everyday Life:

- Embrace Mistakes: Instead of fearing mistakes, see them as opportunities for growth. When you stumble, reflect, learn, and adapt.

- Patience with Self: Recognize that wisdom isn't an overnight acquisition; it's a journey. Being patient with oneself during periods of "folly" can pave the way to deeper insights.

- Open-mindedness: Be open to unconventional paths and methods. What seems like folly today might be viewed as revolutionary wisdom tomorrow.

Proverb 19: "Folly is the cloak of knavery."

Analysis:

This proverb hints at the idea that foolishness or seemingly senseless behavior can often be a disguise or cover for deceit and cunning actions. It warns of the deceptive nature of appearances, suggesting that what might seem foolish on the surface might have a more calculated motive beneath.

Interpretation:

- Deception Behind the Disguise: Just as a cloak conceals what's underneath, folly can serve as a shield to hide deceit or cunning strategies.

- Underestimating Appearances: The proverb advises caution, suggesting that one shouldn't underestimate or dismiss someone or something simply because it appears foolish or insignificant.

- Challenge to Surface Judgments: It pushes readers to delve deeper and not make judgments based solely on outer appearances or superficial behavior.

Neville Goddard's Perspective:

- Hidden Motives: Goddard might propose that the "folly" or outer actions people exhibit are a reflection of their inner beliefs or states, hinting at deeper motives or desires.

- Creation of Reality: Goddard might argue that even if an individual cloaks their desires in folly, these inner beliefs will still shape their external reality.

Application to Everyday Life:

- Look Beyond Appearances: When interacting with others or assessing situations, delve deeper. Look beyond surface behaviors to understand the underlying motives or realities.

- Beware of Manipulation: Recognize that sometimes, individuals might use folly or absurdity as a strategy to mislead or divert attention from their true intentions.

- Inner Truths: Reflect on your actions and behaviors. Understand the beliefs or motives driving them, ensuring they align with your true desires and intentions.

Proverb 20: "Shame is pride's cloak."

Analysis:

This proverb offers a nuanced insight into human emotions, suggesting that shame often serves as a protective layer for our underlying pride. While pride is an acknowledgment of one's self-worth and capabilities, it can be vulnerable. In moments of failure or perceived inadequacy, shame becomes the immediate, protective response to shield that inherent pride.

Interpretation:

- Duality of Emotions: Both pride and shame are two sides of the same coin. While pride celebrates our achievements and self-worth, shame emerges when that pride feels threatened or diminished.

- Defensive Mechanism: Shame, in this context, is a way for the ego to defend itself against external criticisms, ensuring that our internal pride remains intact.

- Complex Human Psyche: The proverb underscores the intricate interplay of human emotions and how they are often layered and intertwined, one hiding or morphing into another.

Neville Goddard's Perspective:

- Internal States: Goddard would argue that our feelings of shame and pride both arise from our internal beliefs about ourselves. When these beliefs are shaken, shame becomes a mechanism to defend our core self-worth.

- Manifested Realities: Goddard might emphasize that continuously cloaking our pride with shame can manifest in our external realities, shaping our experiences based on these dominant emotions.

Application to Everyday Life:

- Self-Reflection: Recognize when you're feeling shame and try to understand its root. Is it genuinely a response to an external event, or is it a protective response to shield your pride?

- Embrace Vulnerability: While it's natural to feel pride, it's also okay to be vulnerable and accept moments of perceived failure or inadequacy without resorting to shame as a defense.

- Growth Through Understanding: By understanding the dynamic between pride and shame, one can navigate emotional responses better, fostering growth and self-awareness.

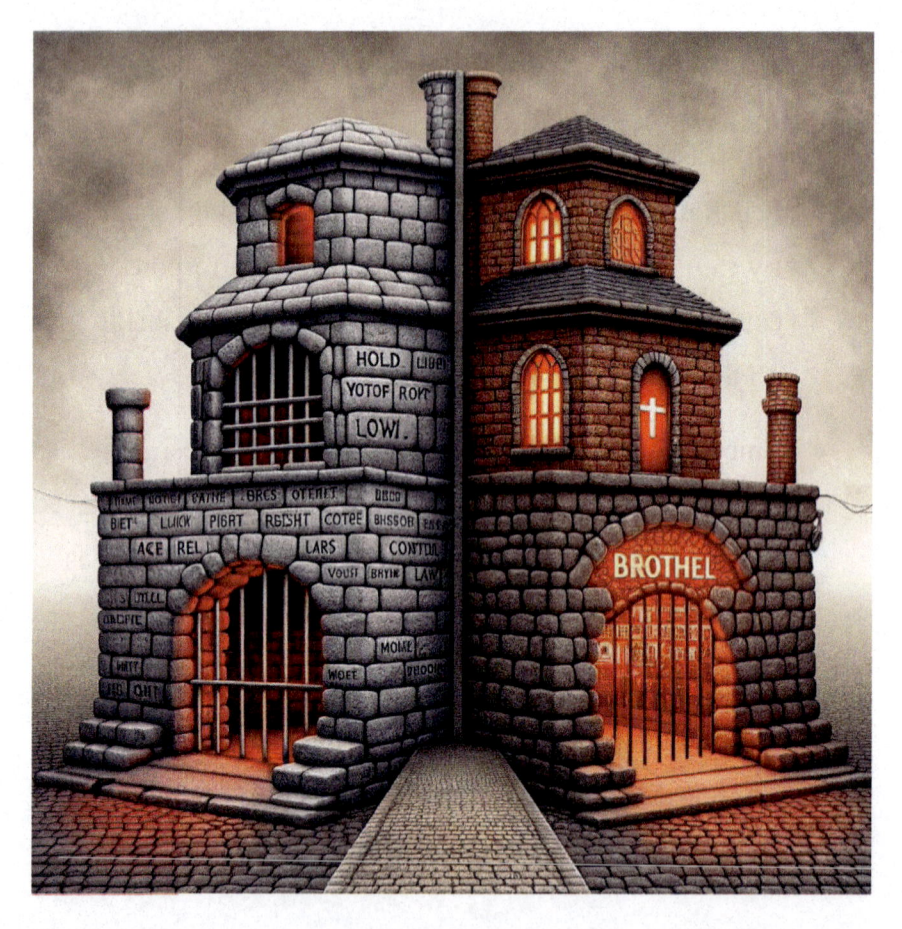

Proverb 21: "Prisons are built with stones of law and brothels with bricks of religion."

Analysis:

This is a potent proverb that draws a stark comparison between institutions (prisons and brothels) and their foundational elements (law and religion). The proverb critiques how societal constructs, particularly law and religion, can be misused to create oppressive or

The Alchemy of Vision

morally ambiguous environments.

Interpretation:

- Institutions & Their Foundations: The proverb suggests that prisons, which represent punishment and control, are built upon the rigidity and strictness of the law. Similarly, brothels, representing indulgence and moral flexibility, are ironically constructed upon religious beliefs, which are typically associated with moral strictness.

- Critical Look at Power Structures: The proverb challenges societal norms, suggesting that what we perceive as just (law) and pure (religion) can be manipulated to serve darker purposes or consequences.

- Perversion of Noble Intentions: It highlights how good intentions or noble ideas can be twisted and exploited for undesirable outcomes.

Neville Goddard's Perspective:

- Inner Beliefs & External Reality: Goddard might suggest that these institutions (prisons and brothels) manifest from our collective beliefs and understanding of law and religion. It's our collective consciousness that shapes the way we interpret and utilize these concepts in our physical world.

- Reflection of Society's State: Both the strictness of law and the indulgences shielded by religion can reflect society's inner states and desires.

Application to Everyday Life:

- Questioning Established Norms: This proverb encourages us to critically examine the societal constructs we live within and question their foundational beliefs. It pushes us to reconsider our blind acceptance of established norms.

- Moral Introspection: Reflect on how personal beliefs align with societal constructs. Are there areas where you see hypocrisy or incongruence?

- Advocacy & Change: If you identify systems or beliefs that appear misaligned with their intended purpose, consider ways to advocate for change or reformation.

The Alchemy of Vision

Proverb 22: "The pride of the peacock is the glory of God."

Analysis:

This proverb draws attention to the majestic display of the peacock's feathers, using it as a metaphor for divine beauty and the celebration of life's grandeur. It touches on the theme of nature as a reflection of the divine.

Interpretation:

- Nature's Splendor as Divine Manifestation: The peacock, with its magnificent plumage, doesn't display its feathers out of vanity but as an intrinsic part of its nature. This natural spectacle is likened to God's glory, suggesting that what might be seen as 'pride' in the animal kingdom is, in fact, a testament to God's craftsmanship.

- Reframing of Pride: In human society, pride is often viewed negatively and associated with arrogance. However, this proverb offers a fresh perspective, suggesting that there's a form of pride that isn't tainted by ego but is instead a genuine expression of one's true nature or God-given gifts.

- Natural vs. Human World: The proverb implicitly contrasts the authentic, uninhibited displays in nature with the often contrived and ego-driven displays of humans.

Neville Goddard's Perspective:

- Inner Beauty Manifested Outwardly: Goddard would likely view the peacock's display as an external manifestation of its inner state, much as our realities reflect our inner beliefs and feelings. The peacock's pride, in its purest form, mirrors the inner beauty and glory of God.

- Celebration of One's True Self: Just as the peacock displays

The Alchemy of Vision

its feathers without inhibition, individuals should embrace and display their true selves, understanding that their unique qualities are a reflection of the divine.

Application to Everyday Life:

- Embracing Authenticity: Take a lesson from the peacock and proudly embrace who you truly are. Understand that being genuine and authentic and taking pride in that is a form of reverence to the higher powers or the universe.

- Acknowledging Natural Beauty: In the world around us, we recognize and appreciate natural beauty as a testament to a greater force or design.

- Redefining Pride: Reconsider the notion of pride. Instead of associating it solely with arrogance, understand that there's a form of pride rooted in genuine self-appreciation and acknowledgment of one's gifts.

Proverb 23: "The lust of the goat is the bounty of God."

Analysis:

This proverb delves into the theme of natural desires and instincts, suggesting that what might be seen as 'base' or 'sinful' by societal standards can be a gift or bounty from a higher power. It challenges societal and religious judgments about natural inclinations.

Interpretation:

- Natural Instincts as Divine Gifts: Goats are known for their strong reproductive instincts, symbolizing raw, untamed natural drives. By linking this "lust" to God's bounty, the proverb implies that even these primal urges come from a divine source.

- Challenge to Societal Morality: Societal and religious norms often label certain desires as sinful or wrong. However, this proverb suggests that these natural inclinations have a place in the grand design and are not inherently evil.

- Holistic View of Creation: Every aspect of nature, even those deemed undesirable by humans, is part of the divine blueprint.

Neville Goddard's Perspective:

- Embracing All Facets of Creation: Goddard would likely interpret the proverb as a call to embrace and understand all aspects of creation, recognizing that every part has its purpose in the grand scheme of things. Denying or suppressing parts of our nature can hinder our spiritual growth.

- Desire as a Catalyst: For Goddard, desires drive our imaginations and shape our realities. Thus, even primal desires can be seen as catalysts for manifesting our destinies.

Application to Everyday Life:

- Understanding Desires: Rather than suppressing or feeling guilty about natural desires, seek to understand them and their place in your life. Recognize that these desires can be channeled positively.

- Challenging Moral Absolutes: Reevaluate societal or religious teachings that label certain natural inclinations as wrong. It's crucial to form one's own understanding and relationship with one's instincts.

- Harmony with Nature: Embrace a more harmonious relationship with nature, understanding that every creature and instinct has its place and purpose.

Proverb 24: "The wrath of the lion is the wisdom of God."

Analysis:

This proverb taps into the raw power and primal nature of the lion, emphasizing the interplay between fierce emotions and divine understanding. It challenges preconceptions about anger and power, suggesting they have a place within divine wisdom.

The Alchemy of Vision

Interpretation:

- Raw Power as Divine Wisdom: The lion, a symbol of strength, majesty, and raw power, embodies natural instincts and primal reactions. By equating the lion's wrath with God's wisdom, the proverb conveys that even fierce emotions can be part of a larger divine plan or understanding.

- Reevaluating Anger: While anger is often viewed negatively, the proverb suggests it has a role in the grand scheme of things, possibly as a force for change or a catalyst for growth.

- Nature's Balance: Every emotion, even those deemed challenging, has a purpose and a role in nature's balance. This proverb underscores that balance.

Neville Goddard's Perspective:

- Anger as a Tool for Growth: Goddard may interpret the proverb to imply that strong emotions, like anger, can be used as tools for personal growth and transformation if harnessed correctly.

- Manifestation of Inner Beliefs: For Goddard, our external world is a reflection of our inner beliefs. The wrath of the lion could represent the manifestation of deeply held convictions, passions, or desires.

Application to Everyday Life:

- Channeling Emotions: Instead of suppressing intense emotions like anger, learn to channel them productively, recognizing their potential as catalysts for change or growth.

- Understanding the Role of Anger: Reevaluate societal perceptions of anger. Instead of viewing it purely negatively, consider its potential for spurring action and inducing positive change when used wisely.

- Embracing All Facets of Emotion: All emotions, even challenging ones, are part of the human experience. Recognizing and understanding them can lead to personal growth and greater emotional intelligence.

Proverb 25: "The nakedness of woman is the work of God."

Analysis:

This proverb addresses the raw beauty and naturalness of the female form, emphasizing its divine origin. It suggests an appreciation of the intrinsic worth and sanctity of the human body, challenging societal taboos and perceptions associated with nudity.

Interpretation:

- Inherent Beauty and Purity: By describing the female form as the work of God, the proverb elevates it to a status of reverence and admiration, emphasizing its natural and divine beauty.

- Challenging Societal Views: In many societies, nudity, especially female nudity, is laden with taboos and judgments. This proverb challenges those views, proposing a more accepting and celebratory perspective.
- Nature vs. Man-Made Constructs: The proverb contrasts the natural state of being (nakedness) with the cultural and religious constructs that have labeled it as shameful or taboo.

Neville Goddard's Perspective:

- Acceptance and Reverence: Goddard, with his emphasis on the power of beliefs and the inner self, might suggest that the proverb calls for a deeper acceptance of oneself and others, recognizing the divinity within.
- Manifestation of Divine Beauty: Just as our reality is a reflection of our inner beliefs, the beauty of the human form can be seen as a manifestation of divine creation.

Application to Everyday Life:

- Body Positivity: Embrace and appreciate the natural beauty of the human body in all its forms. Challenge societal norms that stigmatize or objectify.

- Redefining Beauty Standards: Move away from narrow, man-made beauty standards and acknowledge the inherent and divine beauty present in all individuals.

- Celebration of Life and Creation: Recognize the sanctity of life and the marvel of creation, cherishing every aspect, including the physical form.

Proverb 26: "Excess of sorrow, laughs; excess of joy, weeps."

Analysis:

This proverb delves into the complexities of human emotions, illustrating the fine line between extreme states of feelings and their unexpected manifestations. It speaks to the cyclical and interconnected nature of intense emotions.

Interpretation:

- Paradox of Emotions: The proverb presents an intriguing paradox, suggesting that when sorrow is at its peak, it can manifest as laughter, and overwhelming joy might find its outlet in tears.

- Transitory Nature of Emotions: The sentiment here is the transient nature of emotions. What starts as an intense feeling of one kind can soon turn into its opposite, showcasing the fluidity of human experiences.

The Alchemy of Vision

- Depth of Feelings: It signifies that at the height of an emotion, the boundaries blur. Extreme happiness or sorrow may often have similar expressions, highlighting the depth and intricacy of human feelings.

Neville Goddard's Perspective:

- Inner Reflection: Goddard might view this proverb as a testament to the power of our inner beliefs and feelings. How we feel internally, even if in excess, will always find a way to manifest outwardly, sometimes in unexpected ways.

- Balancing Extremes: Given Goddard's emphasis on the imagination and the belief in desired outcomes, this could signify the need to balance strong emotions, recognizing their power and directing them constructively.

Application to Everyday Life:

- Emotional Awareness: Be cognizant of your emotions, recognizing that they can sometimes manifest in ways that might seem contradictory.

- Embracing All Feelings: It's essential to embrace the full spectrum of emotions without judgment, understanding that our responses might vary based on the depth of what we feel.

- Seek Balance: While it's natural to experience extreme

emotions, finding a balance can help in managing and understanding them better.

<u>Proverb 27: "The roaring of lions, the howling wolves, the raging of the stormy sea, and the destructive sword are portions of eternity too great for the eye of man."</u>

Analysis:

This proverb addresses the vastness and intensity of nature and existence, emphasizing that there are forces and phenomena beyond human comprehension. It brings to light the idea that mankind, though central to its own narrative, is but a small piece in the grand tapestry of the universe.

Interpretation:

- Majesty of Nature: The proverb paints a vivid picture of raw, untamed nature – lions, wolves, and stormy seas – symbolizing the immense power and grandeur that the world possesses.

- Limitations of Human Perception: The "eye of man" here represents human understanding and perception, suggesting that some aspects of existence are too vast or intense to be fully grasped.

- Humility Amidst the Grandeur: There's an underlying tone that humanity should remain humble, acknowledging the

The Alchemy of Vision

limitations in its understanding of the larger cosmos.

Neville Goddard's Perspective:

- Eternal Forces at Play: Goddard would perhaps see these formidable natural forces as representations of the infinite power of imagination and the spiritual realm. They symbolize aspects of the divine that are beyond mere human understanding but can be tapped into through faith and belief.

- Respect for the Infinite: Goddard's teachings on the boundless potential within each individual might align with the proverb's essence, emphasizing respect for the infinite and the eternal forces at play.

Application to Everyday Life:

- Acknowledging Limitations: Recognize that, as humans, our understanding has limits. Embracing this can lead to a deeper respect for the mysteries and vastness of existence.

- Finding Awe in Nature: Let the majesty of nature serve as a reminder of the grandeur of existence, instilling a sense of awe and wonder.

- Seeking Deeper Understanding: While we might not grasp everything, it's essential to remain curious, seeking to understand and connect with the world beyond our immediate perception.

Proverb 28: "The fox condemns the trap, not himself."

Analysis:

This proverb touches upon the theme of personal responsibility and external blame. It delves into the psychology of deflecting blame and not taking ownership of one's actions or decisions.

The Alchemy of Vision

Interpretation:

- External Blame: Using the analogy of a fox, the proverb implies that individuals often blame external factors (the trap) for their dilemmas rather than accepting personal responsibility.

- Cunning and Deception: Foxes are traditionally seen as cunning creatures. Here, the fox's cunning is redirected towards self-deception.

- Avoidance of Accountability: The larger message might be about society's tendency to avoid taking responsibility for its actions, always looking for external culprits.

Neville Goddard's Perspective:

- Inner Reflection: Goddard emphasized the power of the individual's imagination and beliefs in shaping reality. He would likely interpret this proverb as a reminder that external circumstances reflect inner beliefs. Thus, blaming external factors without introspection is counterproductive.

- Creation of Reality: For Goddard, everything in our external world is a manifestation of our inner beliefs. If one finds themselves repeatedly in adverse situations (traps), it might be a call for inner reflection and change.

Application to Everyday Life:

- Taking Ownership: Before blaming external circumstances, it's essential to introspect and determine if personal actions or beliefs contributed to the situation.

- Mindful Living: Cultivate an awareness of personal beliefs and patterns, understanding how they shape experiences.

- Empowerment Through Responsibility: Recognizing one's role in their experiences can be empowering, as it implies the ability to change and create different outcomes.

Proverb 29: "Joys impregnate. Sorrows bring forth."

Analysis:

This proverb delves into the intricate relationship between joy and sorrow, asserting that moments of happiness can give birth to moments of sorrow and vice versa. It's a reflection on the cyclical nature of emotions and experiences.

Interpretation:

- Duality of Emotions: Life is a mixture of highs and lows, and both joy and sorrow play their part. One often leads to the other in a continuous loop of experiences.

- Seeds of Experience: Just as joys can plant the seeds for future sorrows, so can sorrows set the stage for future joys.

- Transient Nature of Emotions: The proverb emphasizes the impermanence of feelings, suggesting that neither extreme is permanent.

Neville Goddard's Perspective:

- Manifestation of Beliefs: Goddard would likely view joys and sorrows as manifestations of our inner beliefs and state. If one is experiencing sorrow, it might have its roots in a past joy or belief, and vice versa.

- Power of Imagination: For Goddard, our imagination plays a vital role in shaping our experiences. This proverb might be a call to be mindful of what we imagine and believe as it will manifest in our lives.

Application to Everyday Life:

- Acceptance of Emotions: Understand that both joy and sorrow are natural parts of life. By embracing both, one can navigate life with a more balanced perspective.

- Mindfulness: Being aware of our current emotional state and its origins can help in managing emotions more effectively.

- Growth Through Experience:* Use both joyous and sorrowful experiences as opportunities for personal growth and understanding.

Proverb 30: "Let man wear the fell of the lion, woman the fleece of the sheep."

Analysis:

This proverb touches upon traditional roles and expectations associated with masculinity and femininity, hinting at the strengths, attributes, and societal impositions each gender has historically faced.

Interpretation:

- Traditional Roles: The lion, often seen as a symbol of strength, courage, and dominance, is associated with man. The sheep, representing gentleness, conformity, and nurturing, is linked with women. The proverb hints at society's conventional expectations.

- Strength and Gentleness: It may also suggest that each gender has its unique strength—man in his assertiveness and woman in her nurturing qualities.

- Questioning Conformity: In Blake's style, there might be a subtle challenge to these norms, urging readers to question and redefine these traditional roles.

Neville Goddard's Perspective:

- Inner States: Goddard would probably interpret this not as a gendered statement but as representative of different states of consciousness. The lion might represent a state of confidence, assertion, and creation, while the sheep symbolizes receptivity, faith, and acceptance.

- Balancing Forces: Both "lion" and "sheep" attributes are necessary for manifesting desires: the assertive force to plant a desire and the receptive faith to allow its manifestation.

Application to Everyday Life:

- Redefining Roles: Challenge societal norms and traditional roles. Understand that both "lion" and "sheep" qualities are present in everyone, regardless of gender.

- Embracing Dualities: Recognize and harness the power of both assertiveness (lion) and receptivity (sheep) in personal growth and manifestations.

- Personal Identity: Define oneself not by societal expectations but by personal attributes, beliefs, and desires.

Proverb 31: "The bird a nest, the spider a web, man friendship."

Analysis:

This proverb delves into the inherent nature of different creatures and how they seek shelter, safety, or connection. For birds, it's a nest; for spiders, a web; and for humans, it's the bond of friendship.

Interpretation:

- Natural Instincts: Just as birds instinctively build nests and spiders weave webs, humans are innately driven to seek and nurture friendships.

- Safety and Shelter: While nests and webs offer physical protection and means of sustenance for birds and spiders, respectively, friendship offers emotional and psychological refuge for humans.

- Questioning Solitude: Blake's rebellious spirit might also be a critique against isolation and societal constructs that prevent genuine connection.

Neville Goddard's Perspective:

- Inner Connection: For Goddard, everything external mirrors an internal state. Friendship might be seen as an external reflection of our inner connection to all of humanity and to the divine imagination.

- Manifesting Relationships: Just as we manifest our realities, the relationships we nurture are reflections of our inner beliefs about ourselves and the world.

Application to Everyday Life:

- Value of Relationships: Recognize the fundamental human

need for connection and the profound impact friendships can have on our well-being.

- Nurturing Bonds: Just as a bird meticulously builds its nest and a spider its web, invest time and care in cultivating meaningful friendships.

- Reflection and Growth: Friendships can serve as mirrors, reflecting our strengths, areas for growth, and deeply held beliefs. Embrace them for personal introspection and growth.

Proverb 32: "The selfish, smiling fool and the sullen, frowning fool shall be both thought wise, that they may be a rod."

Analysis:

This proverb speaks to the misperceptions of society, where outward expressions or appearances are sometimes mistaken for genuine wisdom or knowledge. It comments on the ease with which people can be deceived by superficial cues.

Interpretation:

- Mistaken Wisdom: Both the outwardly cheerful fool and the seemingly contemplative fool are perceived as wise not due to actual intelligence but due to their exterior demeanor.

- Society's Facade: Blake might be hinting at the artificial nature of societal judgments and how easy it is to misjudge based on surface-level interpretations.

- The Rod: The rod, traditionally a symbol of power or authority, might imply that these 'fools' are given undue power or influence based on these mistaken perceptions.

Neville Goddard's Perspective:

- External vs. Internal Reality: Goddard often emphasized the importance of internal beliefs over external appearances. This proverb aligns with that perspective, pointing out the folly in judging based on the external alone.

- Manifestation of Belief: If society believes and elevates these fools due to their demeanor, it's a manifestation of society's shallow values.

Application to Everyday Life:

- Look Beyond the Surface: It's essential to dive deeper and understand a person's true nature rather than relying on first impressions or superficial judgments.

- Challenge Conformity: Don't accept societal norms or values without questioning. Look for genuine wisdom and knowledge rather than accepting pretense.

- Guard Against Deception: Recognize that appearances can

deceive and that it's crucial to develop discernment.

Proverb 33: "What is now proved, was once only imagined."

Analysis:

This proverb speaks to the power of imagination and the evolution of knowledge. It underscores the notion that today's truths and certainties often began as mere thoughts or ideas in the past.

Interpretation:

- Evolution of Ideas: Every discovery, invention, or understanding we have today was once a mere idea or a hypothesis in someone's mind. It's through exploration, questioning, and testing that imaginations become realities.

- Power of Imagination: Blake emphasizes that imagination isn't just fantasy but a precursor to reality. It serves as the birthplace of innovation.

- Limitless Potential: The statement hints at the endless possibilities of human thought and how our perceptions of reality and truth are ever-evolving.

Neville Goddard's Perspective:

- Creation through Imagination: Goddard believed that imagination is the foundation of creation. Everything we witness in the external world began as an imaginative act.

This proverb would resonate deeply with his teachings.

- Manifestation of Reality: For Goddard, imagining something vividly and with feeling is the first step towards its manifestation in the physical world. Thus, what is proven today was first intensely felt and believed in the realm of imagination.

Application to Everyday Life:

- Value of Dreams: Don't dismiss your dreams and aspirations as mere fantasies. With belief and action, they can evolve into tangible realities.

- Encourage Imagination: Allow yourself to think outside the box and imagine without constraints. Today's wildest thoughts can be tomorrow's breakthroughs.

- Never Stop Exploring: Recognize that our understanding of the world is not static. Continuously question, learn, and innovate.

Proverb 34: The rat, the mouse, the fox, the rabbit, watch the roots; the lion, the tiger, the horse, the elephant, watch the fruits."

Analysis:

This proverb delves into the concept of natural hierarchy and inherent instincts. Through the imagery of animals and their food habits, it provides insights into behavior, priorities, and the circle of life.

Interpretation:

- Diverse Priorities: Just as different animals focus on different food sources based on their nature and size, humans too have varied focuses in life based on their capacities and environments.

- Natural Instincts: Every creature, including humans, has inherent tendencies and instincts. Understanding and aligning with them leads to harmony.

- Hierarchy of Needs: In the broader picture, it speaks to the idea that smaller concerns (roots) are the purview of smaller entities, while larger entities focus on bigger rewards (fruits).

Neville Goddard's Perspective:

- Individual Desires: Goddard might see this as a reflection of individual desires and states of consciousness. Every person operates based on their beliefs and desires, much like animals act on their instincts.

- Manifestation based on Focus: Just as animals manifest their sustenance by focusing on their natural food source, humans, too, manifest their realities based on where they place their focus and belief.

Application to Everyday Life:

- Recognize Your Focus: Understand where you are directing your energy and attention. Are you focusing on the basics (roots) or aiming higher (fruits)?

- Align with Your Instincts: Follow your natural inclinations and strengths. Trying to act against your nature can lead to dissatisfaction.

- Respect Diversity: Just as different animals have different roles in the ecosystem, each individual has a unique path. It's essential to respect and understand the diverse perspectives and focuses of others.

Proverb 35: "The cistern contains; the fountain overflows."

Analysis:

This proverb contrasts the nature of containment and abundance. Using the imagery of a cistern and a fountain, it delves deep into the concepts of limitations versus limitless potential and the dichotomy between static and dynamic forces.

Interpretation:

- Limitation vs. Limitlessness: A cistern, though holding water, has a set capacity. On the other hand, a fountain symbolizes constant movement and an unending source. This can be likened to a mindset of scarcity versus one of abundance.

- Static vs. Dynamic: The cistern represents something static, a reservoir that retains but does not add, while the fountain represents continuous flow and dynamism.
- Inward vs. Outward Expression: While the cistern signifies internal storage, the fountain is expressive and shares its bounty with the world, symbolizing generosity and external manifestation.

Neville Goddard's Perspective:

- Inner Abundance: For Goddard, the fountain could signify the endless creative potential within us. When we tap into our imagination and believe in our desires, we overflow with possibilities, much like the fountain.
- Limitations of the Physical: The cistern might be seen as the physical world, limited and defined, while the overflowing fountain represents the boundless spiritual world, reflecting our infinite imaginative capabilities.

Application to Everyday Life:

- Mindset Shift: Recognize if you're operating from a mindset of scarcity (cistern) or one of abundance (fountain). Shifting to an abundance mindset can change your perspective and approach to life's challenges.

- Continuous Growth: Aim to be like the fountain, continuously learning, evolving, and sharing your wisdom and experiences.

- Generosity: Embrace the spirit of giving and sharing. Like the fountain that doesn't hold back its waters, be generous with your knowledge, love, and resources.

Proverb 36: "One thought fills immensity."

Analysis:

This proverb captures the vastness and profound impact of a single thought. It emphasizes the idea that thoughts, though intangible, possess immense power and can shape the vast expanse of our lives and realities.

Interpretation:

- Magnitude of Thoughts: Just as a drop of ink can spread in water, a single thought can ripple through our consciousness and influence our actions, feelings, and entire life trajectories.

- Infinite Potential: The proverb suggests that thoughts aren't confined by physical limitations. Their influence and reach are boundless.

- Universality: A single idea or realization can resonate with and be understood by countless individuals across cultures and times, proving the universality of certain truths and experiences.

Neville Goddard's Perspective:

- Creative Power: Goddard emphasized the creative power of imagination and belief. He would probably interpret this proverb as an affirmation of how one thought, when truly believed and felt, can manifest and fill the entirety of one's world.

- Internal Reflects External: In Goddard's teachings, the outer world is a reflection of our inner beliefs and thoughts. Thus, one dominant thought can shape our external reality.

Application to Everyday Life:

- Mindfulness: Be aware of your thoughts. Given their potential impact, it's crucial to nurture positive and empowering beliefs.

- Change Starts Within: If you wish to change aspects of your life, start by altering your dominant thoughts. Embrace those that align with your desired reality.

- Universal Connection: Recognize that your profound realizations, though personal, can resonate with others. Sharing them can create bridges of understanding and connection.

Proverb 37: "Always be ready to speak your mind, and a base man will avoid you."

Analysis:

This proverb underscores the power of authenticity and the value of standing firm in one's convictions. By being genuine and voicing our beliefs, we act as a natural deterrent to those who might harbor deceitful intentions or who are not aligned with our core principles.

Interpretation:

- Authenticity as a Shield: When one consistently speaks their mind, it becomes a protective barrier, discouraging dishonest or insincere individuals from approaching.

- Value of Honesty: There's an implicit value placed on honest communication and integrity in this proverb. Speaking one's mind becomes a mark of character.

- Repelling Disharmony: The proverb suggests that by being true to oneself, one can naturally repel those who might

The Alchemy of Vision

bring discord or negativity.

Neville Goddard's Perspective:

- Internal Congruence: For Goddard, the outer world mirrors our inner state. Being genuine and forthright in expressing oneself ensures that one's internal beliefs and external reality are in alignment.

- Attraction and Manifestation: Goddard might argue that by speaking your mind and maintaining authenticity, you're setting clear intentions and thereby attracting circumstances and individuals in harmony with your genuine self.

Application to Everyday Life:

- Embrace Authenticity: In relationships, work, and personal endeavors, strive to be genuine and forthright. This not only attracts like-minded individuals but also discourages dishonest ones.

- Voice Your Convictions: Don't shy away from sharing your beliefs, even if they're unpopular. Standing by your convictions can garner respect from others.

- Filter Through Authenticity: By being genuine, you naturally filter out those who aren't aligned with your values, leading to more harmonious and meaningful connections.

MYCHAEL T. RENN

Proverb 38: "Everything possible to be believed is an image of truth."

Analysis:

This proverb delves into the realm of perception, suggesting that beliefs, even if diverse or seemingly fantastical, have a kernel of truth to them. It implies that our convictions and understandings, regardless of how varied they might be, stem from some aspect of reality or genuine experience.

Interpretation:

- Subjectivity of Truth: The saying posits that truth isn't monolithic. What one person sees as true, based on their experiences and understanding, might differ from another's perspective, yet both are valid.

- Infinite Realities: In a vast universe, myriad experiences and perceptions can coexist, each forming its own version of truth.

- Validation of Belief: The proverb respects and validates individual beliefs, suggesting that they all have their place in the tapestry of existence.

Neville Goddard's Perspective:

- Manifested Beliefs: Goddard emphasized that our beliefs

The Alchemy of Vision

shape our reality. This proverb aligns with that, suggesting that what we believe deeply, we can manifest or at least perceive in our reality.

- Imaginative Creation: Goddard might interpret this as a nod to the power of imagination and belief in shaping one's experience and reality.

Application to Everyday Life:

- Open-mindedness: Approach others' beliefs with respect and curiosity, understanding that their truths stem from their unique experiences and perceptions.

- Personal Validation: Trust in your convictions and understand that your beliefs, experiences, and truths are valid, even if they differ from the mainstream.

- Exploration of Reality: Use this as an invitation to explore different philosophies, cultures, and worldviews, recognizing the inherent truth within each.

Proverb 39: "The eagle never lost so much time as when he submitted to learn of the crow."

Analysis:

This proverb speaks to the importance of discerning who we learn from and the value of understanding one's own strengths and capabilities. It suggests that time is wasted when we do not recognize or appreciate our own innate talents and instead try to gain from those whose abilities do not match or exceed our own.

Interpretation:

- **Valuing Self-Potential**: The eagle, known for its majesty and power, symbolizes excellence and high capability. When it stoops to learn from the crow, a bird considered of lesser majesty, it's seen as misjudging its own superior capacities.

- **Choosing Mentors Wisely**: It stresses the importance of choosing teachers or mentors who can genuinely elevate us and from whom we can meaningfully learn, rather than those who might lead us astray or hold us back.

- **Inherent Strength and Independence**: The proverb highlights the importance of recognizing and utilizing one's inherent strengths and being wary of underestimating oneself by comparing or belittling one's capabilities.

Neville Goddard's Perspective:

- **Self-Concept and Achievement**: Goddard might view this as a lesson in understanding and maintaining one's self-concept. He believed strongly in the idea that individuals create their reality through their imagination and self-perception. Thus, an eagle learning from a crow might symbolize someone with great potential limiting themselves by adopting a lesser view of their capabilities.

- **Aspiration and Influence**: It's important, from Goddard's viewpoint, to aspire and align oneself with influences that resonate with one's highest ideals and potential.

Application to Everyday Life:

- **Know Your Worth**: Recognize and cultivate your inherent talents instead of underestimating them. Understand your unique strengths and how to best utilize them.

- **Selective Learning**: Be selective about who you learn from or take advice from, ensuring that it aligns with and elevates your goals and values.

- **Independence and Growth**: Maintain independence in your learning and growth journey, ensuring that the paths you follow and the lessons you undertake are truly beneficial to your personal and professional development.

Proverb 40: "The fox provides for himself, but God provides for the lion."

Analysis:

This proverb juxtaposes the cunning and self-reliance of the fox with the raw power and divine providence of the lion, delving into themes of self-sufficiency versus divine intervention.

The Alchemy of Vision

Interpretation:

- Self-Reliance vs. Divine Providence: The fox, known for its cunning and resourcefulness, is a symbol of those who rely on their own wits to navigate life. The lion, on the other hand, represents those who lean on a higher power or the natural order of things to provide for them.

- Nature of Power: The fox's power lies in its strategy and ability to adapt, while the lion's power is intrinsic, raw, and divinely ordained.

- Challenge of Societal Views: Blake may be subtly commenting on societal attitudes towards the "mighty" (lion) and the "cunning" (fox), asking readers to reflect on their beliefs about power, providence, and self-reliance.

Neville Goddard's Perspective:

- Internal vs. External Creation: Goddard might see the fox as representing those who use their external senses and reasoning to create their reality. The lion, in contrast, would represent those who rely on their inner beliefs and feelings, trusting the universe (or God) to manifest their desires.

- Power of Imagination: Just as the lion is provided for, individuals who recognize and harness the power of their imagination (and thus align with the divine) will find their needs met in seemingly effortless ways.

Application to Everyday Life:

- Know Your Strengths: Understand where your strengths lie. Are you someone who meticulously plans and strategizes like the fox, or do you operate with inherent confidence and faith akin to the lion?

- Trust in the Universe: While it's essential to be proactive and resourceful, also recognize the moments when it's best to let go and trust in a higher power or the flow of life to guide and provide for you.

- Reflect on Power Dynamics: Consider the ways in which society rewards cunning versus inherent power, and think about how this impacts your own views on success and provision.

Proverb 41: "Think in the morning, act in the noon, eat in the evening, sleep in the night."

Analysis:

This proverb speaks to the natural rhythm of a day and suggests an optimal way of structuring one's activities for maximum effectiveness and harmony with nature's cycles.

Interpretation:

- Natural Rhythms: The proverb aligns with the natural progression of a day, urging individuals to flow with the day's energies, from the freshness of morning thoughts to the peaceful rest of the night.

- Intentional Living: The recommendation to think in the morning underscores the importance of starting the day with intention and clarity, laying the groundwork for productive actions later.

- Challenge to Modern Lifestyle: In today's fast-paced world, where work, leisure, and rest often blur together, this proverb serves as a reminder of the benefits of compartmentalizing different activities and aligning them with nature's cadence.

Neville Goddard's Perspective:

- Manifestation Cycle: For Goddard, thinking in the morning could symbolize the planting of seeds of desire. Acting in the noon might signify faith in these desires' manifestation, followed by the nourishment of belief (eating in the evening), culminating in peaceful trust and surrender during sleep, where imagination does its work.

- Power of Rest: The emphasis on sleep is crucial for Goddard, as he believed that sleep was a time when our subconscious could most effectively be influenced by our desires and beliefs.

Application to Everyday Life:

- Mindful Structuring: Structure your day in alignment with this proverb, setting aside specific times for contemplation, action, nourishment, and rest.

- Embrace Natural Cycles: Recognize the importance of aligning with nature's rhythms for overall well-being and productivity.

- Reclaim Your Night: In a world filled with distractions and endless entertainment, prioritize restful sleep to rejuvenate your mind and body.

Proverb 42: "He who has suffered you to impose on him knows you."

Analysis:

This proverb delves into the dynamics of relationships, trust, and the revealing nature of betrayal. It speaks to the idea that actions and responses in relationships can lead to deeper insights into a person's character.

Interpretation:

- Insights from Betrayal: When someone allows another to deceive or impose upon them, it's often through this act of imposition that the true nature of the deceiver is revealed.

The Alchemy of Vision

- Depth of Understanding: The person imposed upon gains a profound understanding of the imposer's character and motivations, often more than the imposer realizes.

- Challenge to Superficial Relations: Blake's proverb nudges us to be wary of superficial interactions and to understand that deeper truths emerge in times of conflict or betrayal.

Neville Goddard's Perspective:

- Inner Reflection: For Goddard, the external world is a reflection of our inner beliefs. This imposition might symbolize an internal belief or assumption that is being mirrored in one's reality.

- Power of Awareness: Realizing how someone truly is can empower an individual to change their assumptions or beliefs about that person or situation, thus altering their future interactions and manifestations.

Application to Everyday Life:

- Awareness in Relationships: Be attentive to the actions and behaviors of those around you, for they can provide valuable insights into their true nature.

- Learning from Experiences: Instead of lamenting over betrayals or impositions, use them as opportunities to understand others better and adjust your future interactions.

- Valuing Authenticity: Foster genuine relationships based on mutual respect and understanding, avoiding those who seek to deceive or impose.

Proverb 43: "As the plow follows words, so God rewards prayers."

Analysis:

This proverb juxtaposes the tangible, earthly act of plowing with the ethereal, spiritual act of praying, suggesting a direct cause-and-effect relationship between effort and reward, both in the material and spiritual realms.

Interpretation:

- Effort and Outcome: Just as the plow creates a furrow in response to the farmer's guidance, so does a prayer generate a response from the divine. Both actions—plowing and praying—require intent and effort to yield results.

- Manifestation of Intent: Words guide the plow, shaping the earth to the farmer's will. Similarly, prayers are the words that communicate our desires and intentions to the divine.

- Direct Reciprocity: The proverb implies a direct relationship: the more sincere and dedicated the effort (whether it's plowing or praying), the greater the reward.

The Alchemy of Vision

Neville Goddard's Perspective:

- Conscious Creation: Goddard believed in the power of imagination and feeling in manifesting desires. Prayers, for him, are not just words but feelings and beliefs. When one prays with genuine emotion and belief, the universe (or God) responds in kind.

- External Reflection of Internal Beliefs: The rewards received are a direct reflection of our internal state during prayer. As one truly believes and feels, so shall they receive.

Application to Everyday Life:

- Purposeful Actions: Whether in work or in spiritual practices, the effort and intent behind our actions determine the outcome. It's not just about going through the motions but genuinely investing in them.

- Faith in the Process: Just as a farmer has faith that his efforts will yield a crop, we should have faith that our sincere prayers and efforts will manifest the results we desire.

- Patience and Persistence: Like farming, the results of our efforts (or prayers) might not be immediate. It's essential to be patient and persistent, trusting that the rewards will come in due time.

Proverb 44: "The tigers of wrath are wiser than the horses of instruction."

Analysis:

This provocative proverb juxtaposes two powerful images: the fierce, untamed tiger and the disciplined, domesticated horse. It delves into the interplay between raw emotion and structured learning, advocating for the inherent wisdom found in passion and intuition.

Interpretation:

- Raw Emotion vs. Formal Instruction: The "tigers of wrath" symbolize strong emotions, passion, and instinct, while the "horses of instruction" represent formal education, discipline, and societal teachings.

- Valuing Intuition: The proverb suggests that there's a deeper wisdom in trusting one's instincts and emotions than merely relying on structured learning or societal norms.

- Questioning Conformity: In line with Blake's overarching themes, this proverb can be seen as a challenge to societal conventions and the traditional education system.

Neville Goddard's Perspective:

- Emotional Realism: Goddard emphasized the power of

feeling in manifesting desires. The "tigers of wrath" might be interpreted as those strong emotions that, when felt deeply, can shape our reality more potently than mere learned instructions or affirmations.

- Power of Passion: Goddard would likely argue that it's our passionate beliefs and feelings, even more than our learned knowledge, that shape our world.

Application to Everyday Life:

- Trust Your Gut: While education and learning are invaluable, there are moments when it's wise to trust our instincts, passions, and emotions.

- Challenge the Status Quo: Don't accept teachings or instructions at face value. Instead, question them, and if your inner "tiger" feels differently, honor that intuition.

- Harnessing Emotion: Emotions, even intense ones like wrath, can be channeled productively. They can provide insight, drive, and a deeper understanding than mere instruction can offer.

Proverb 45: "Expect poison from standing water."

Analysis:

This proverb utilizes the metaphor of stagnant water to communicate a profound lesson about stagnation, complacency, and the potential dangers of inertia in our lives.

Interpretation:

The Alchemy of Vision

- Dangers of Stagnation: Just as standing water can become a breeding ground for harmful bacteria and disease, being stagnant in life—whether in thoughts, beliefs, or actions—can lead to negativity or deterioration.

- Value of Flow and Change: The opposite of standing water is flowing water, which stays fresh and pure. This can be seen as a metaphor for the importance of progress, change, and continuous learning in life.

- Questioning Inertia: True to Blake's style, the proverb challenges us to be wary of societal or personal stagnation and to always seek growth and movement.

Neville Goddard's Perspective:

- Stagnant Beliefs: For Goddard, standing water could symbolize unchallenged and outdated beliefs that hold one back from realizing their true potential. These stagnant beliefs can poison our potential and manifest undesirable outcomes.

- *Refreshing Our Inner World: Goddard would likely advocate for the importance of renewing our beliefs, feelings, and imagination regularly to manifest a positive reality.

Application to Everyday Life:

- Seek Growth: Avoid becoming too complacent in your beliefs, habits, or routines. Embrace change, seek new experiences, and challenge yourself regularly.

- Beware of Negative Environments: Just as stagnant water can be harmful, staying in negative environments or holding onto outdated beliefs can hinder personal growth. Recognize such situations and seek freshness in perspectives and surroundings.

- Value Movement: Whether it's through physical activity, traveling, learning, or simply changing your routine, ensure there's movement in your life to keep your perspectives fresh and vibrant.

<u>Proverb 46: "You never know what is enough unless you know what is more than enough."</u>

Analysis:

This proverb dives into the themes of excess, boundaries, and self-awareness, suggesting that true understanding and appreciation often come from pushing boundaries and occasionally stepping beyond them.

The Alchemy of Vision

Interpretation:

- Understanding Limits: One can only genuinely recognize their limits or what suffices by occasionally experiencing or seeing what goes beyond the acceptable or comfortable boundaries.

- Value of Excess: Sometimes, going into the realms of excess can bring clarity about what is truly essential and balanced in life.

- Challenging Conventions: Consistent with Blake's rebellious spirit, this proverb urges individuals to question societal norms and the arbitrary limits they often set.

Neville Goddard's Perspective:

- Boundaries of Creation: Goddard would interpret this in the light of our imaginative power. By pushing the boundaries of our imagination, even into the realms of excess, we can better understand our true desires and the extent of our creative capabilities.

- Recognizing Abundance: For Goddard, knowing "more than enough" would emphasize the abundance that comes from realizing our imaginal acts, helping us discern between mere satisfaction and true fulfillment.

Application to Everyday Life:

- Risk and Reward: Don't be afraid to step out of your comfort zone. Sometimes, by taking risks and pushing our boundaries, we gain a clearer understanding of our desires and what truly satisfies us.

- Reflection: After moments of excess, take time to reflect on the experience. What did it teach you about your limits, desires, or values?

- Question Societal Standards: Society often sets standards for what is "enough." Challenge these norms and decide for yourself what feels right and balanced.

Proverb 47: "Listen to the fool's reproach; it is a kingly title."

Analysis:

This proverb delves into the idea of wisdom being found in unexpected places and suggests that true leadership or nobility can be reflected in one's ability to listen to even the most scorned or marginalized voices.

Interpretation:

- Valuing All Voices: By urging us to listen to the "fool's reproach," Blake emphasizes the importance of considering all perspectives, even those that society might dismiss or ridicule.

The Alchemy of Vision

- Test of Nobility: A true leader or noble soul is one who remains open-minded, seeking wisdom from all quarters, irrespective of societal hierarchies or biases.

- Rebuking Conventional Wisdom: In line with Blake's penchant for challenging societal norms, this proverb underscores the idea that wisdom isn't exclusive to traditionally revered sources.

Neville Goddard's Perspective:

- Acknowledging All Thoughts: Goddard would emphasize that all thoughts and beliefs, even those perceived as foolish, play a role in shaping our reality. Thus, listening to even the "fool's reproach" can provide insights into one's subconscious beliefs and imaginal acts.

- Value in Reflection: For Goddard, reflecting on any feedback, even if it seems baseless, can provide insights into one's self-conception and the state from which they operate.

Application to Everyday Life:

- Open-Mindedness: Encourage yourself to be receptive to feedback and opinions from all sources. Often, the most unexpected voices bring the most profound insights.

- Self-Reflection: Use criticism or reproach as an opportunity for introspection. Understand where it's coming from, and see if it holds any truth or lessons for personal growth.

- Challenge Societal Biases: Move beyond societal biases that dictate whose voice holds value. Recognize that wisdom and insight can come from the most unexpected places.

Proverb 48: "The eyes of fire, the nostrils of air, the mouth of water, the beard of earth."

Analysis:

This proverb beautifully embodies the elemental interplay and the innate connection between humans and the natural world. It paints a vivid picture of a being synthesized from core elements, suggesting the harmony and interdependence of all life.

Interpretation:

- Unity with Nature: Each body part corresponds to a fundamental element, illustrating that humans are not separate from nature but rather a direct product and manifestation of it.

- Sensory Experiences: The senses - sight, smell, taste, and touch - connect us to the world. Blake might be highlighting the way each sense is linked to an elemental force, emphasizing our sensory bond with nature.

- Interdependence: Just as we depend on these elements for survival, they are also interconnected, highlighting the cyclical and interdependent nature of life.

Neville Goddard's Perspective:

- Manifestation from Elements: Goddard might see this as a representation of how our reality (or our body in this context) is a manifestation formed by our beliefs and feelings. Each element might symbolize different facets of our imaginative acts that shape our world.

- Inner World Shapes the Outer: Just as the elements combine to form a face in Blake's proverb, Goddard emphasizes that our inner beliefs and feelings (our personal "elements") shape our external reality.

Application to Everyday Life:

- Respect for Nature: Recognize our deep-rooted connection with the natural world. This understanding fosters a sense of respect and a need for sustainable interactions with our environment.

- Mindfulness: Being mindful of our sensory experiences can help ground us, making us more present and aware of our surroundings and our connection to the world.

- Holistic Living: By understanding the interconnectedness of all things, we can adopt a more holistic approach to life, ensuring balance and harmony in our actions.

Proverb 49: "The weak in courage is strong in cunning."

Analysis:

This proverb touches upon the adaptive qualities individuals develop when faced with certain disadvantages or challenges. It emphasizes that when traditional strengths may be lacking, other skills or attributes can come to the forefront to compensate.

Interpretation:

- Compensatory Strengths: Not everyone possesses the same kind of strength. Some may lack physical prowess or overt bravery but might have the intellectual capability or strategic thinking to outsmart challenges.

- Survival and Adaptation: This speaks to the idea of survival and how living beings adapt to their circumstances. When one path is closed, another becomes essential for survival.

- Value of Cunning: The proverb suggests that cunning is not a lesser form of strength but an alternative one, and it's just as valuable in certain situations.

The Alchemy of Vision

Neville Goddard's Perspective:

- Inner Strengths Manifesting Externally: Goddard would likely emphasize that our inner beliefs and feelings shape our reality. If someone believes they lack courage, their subconscious may guide them to develop cunning as a coping mechanism or alternative strength.

- Creative Use of Imagination: The use of cunning can be seen as an imaginative act – creating alternative paths or solutions when direct ones are not accessible.

Application to Everyday Life:

- Self-awareness: Understanding and acknowledging one's strengths and weaknesses can lead to more effective problem-solving and navigating challenges in life.

- Redefining Strength: Strength doesn't always manifest as physical prowess or boldness. Sometimes, it's the subtle art of strategy, wit, and cunning that prevails.

- Empathy: Recognizing that everyone has their unique strengths can foster understanding and mutual respect among individuals.

Proverb 50: "The apple tree never asks the beech how he shall grow, nor the lion the horse how he shall take his prey."

Analysis:

This proverb delves into the concept of inherent nature, individuality, and the intrinsic knowledge and intuition that every entity possesses. It sheds light on the idea that one doesn't need to seek external validation or guidance when following one's innate path or instincts.

Interpretation:

- Innate Knowledge and Individuality: Each entity, whether it's a tree or an animal, has its unique mode of existence and growth. They don't rely on others to determine their path, underscoring the idea of trusting oneself.

- Absence of External Validation: The apple tree and the lion are not swayed or influenced by external perspectives. They operate based on their internal compass, emphasizing the insignificance of outside opinions.

- Nature's Authenticity: The natural world is devoid of pretense and comparison, highlighting the purity and genuineness of following one's inherent nature.

Neville Goddard's Perspective:

- Inner Conviction: Goddard would probably infer that our internal convictions and beliefs drive our actions and destinies. Just as the apple tree doesn't need external guidance, individuals should trust their inner visions and feelings.

- Creation from Within: The idea aligns with Goddard's teachings that our external reality mirrors our internal beliefs. Instead of seeking outside, one must cultivate and trust their inner world.

Application to Everyday Life:

- Self-trust: Believe in your abilities and instincts. Often, the answers you seek are within you, waiting to be acknowledged.

- Avoiding Comparison: Every individual's journey is unique. Comparing oneself to others can be counterproductive and detract from one's unique path.

- Embracing Individuality: Celebrate what makes you unique. Recognize that you have your way of approaching life, just as every entity in nature does.

Proverb 51: "The thankful receiver bears a plentiful harvest."

Analysis:

This proverb underscores the significance of gratitude and its potent ability to manifest abundance. Recognizing and appreciating blessings, no matter how small, can create a foundation for more blessings to flourish.

Interpretation:

- Power of Gratitude: A heart filled with gratitude tends to see more opportunities and blessings. Thankfulness acts as a magnifier, amplifying the good in one's life.

- Cycle of Abundance: When one shows genuine appreciation for what they have, they cultivate a positive environment conducive to growth, prosperity, and further blessings.

- Deep Connection: Beyond the material realm, being thankful can deepen one's connection with the universe, higher powers, or others, fostering harmonious relationships.

Neville Goddard's Perspective:

- Emotional Resonance: Goddard would emphasize the vibrational nature of emotions. Feeling thankful aligns individuals with the frequency of abundance, thereby attracting more of what they are grateful for.

- Internal State Reflecting Externally: Gratitude, for Goddard, is a potent state of being. By being thankful internally, one changes their external reality to mirror that

The Alchemy of Vision

internal state of abundance.

Application to Everyday Life:

- Daily Gratitude: Implementing a daily gratitude practice can alter one's perspective, allowing them to focus more on the positive aspects of their life.

- Manifestation through Appreciation: Recognizing and valuing the present helps in manifesting a future filled with even more to be grateful for.

- Positive Interactions: A thankful demeanor can improve interpersonal relationships, as gratitude often breeds kindness, understanding, and positivity.

<u>Proverb 52: "If others had not been foolish, we should have been so."</u>

Analysis:

This proverb reflects on the shared human experience of making mistakes and underscores the idea that observing the errors of others can prevent us from making similar ones. It acknowledges the collective wisdom derived from communal errors.

Interpretation:

- Learning from Others: Throughout history, individuals learn not only from their mistakes but also from the blunders of others. This shared learning experience is essential for collective growth.

- Acknowledgment of Imperfection: The proverb implies that no one is exempt from folly. By observing the errors of others, we might sidestep similar pitfalls, but we'll inevitably encounter our unique challenges.

- Interconnectedness of Experience: Every individual's experience adds to the communal pool of knowledge, allowing subsequent generations to benefit.

Neville Goddard's Perspective:

- External Reflection: For Goddard, the external world mirrors our internal states. Observing others' follies isn't just about learning from their mistakes but understanding that they are reflections of collective consciousness.

- Inner Transformations: By acknowledging and learning from the missteps of others, individuals can change their internal beliefs and assumptions, leading to a shift in their external realities.

Application to Everyday Life:

- Value of Observation: One doesn't always have to experience a mistake firsthand to learn from it. Observing and empathizing with others can offer valuable insights.

- Humility and Growth: Recognizing that everyone is prone to errors promotes humility. Such acknowledgment fosters personal growth, as it encourages continuous learning and adaptation.

- Shared Wisdom: Engaging in conversations about past mistakes without judgment can lead to collective enlightenment and prevent repetitive errors.

Proverb 53: "The soul of sweet delight can never be defiled."

Analysis:

This proverb celebrates the purity and resilience of the human spirit, suggesting that the core essence of joy and delight within us remains untainted, regardless of external circumstances or actions. It speaks to an innate sanctity and beauty within the soul that is perpetual and unassailable.

Interpretation:

- **Inherent Purity**: The phrase "soul of sweet delight" implies a core of goodness and joy inherent to the human spirit. The proverb suggests that this core remains pure and undefiled, regardless of life's trials and tribulations.

- **Resilience of Spirit**: It reflects the idea that the human soul is resilient and maintains its essence of delight and purity, even in the face of adversity or corruption.

- **Sanctity of Joy**: The proverb underscores the idea that true joy or delight has a sanctity to it, a quality that is not easily tarnished or lost. It is a natural, enduring aspect of the human condition.

Neville Goddard's Perspective:

- **Untouched Inner State**: Goddard might view this as an acknowledgment of the untouchable, perfect state of the human imagination and soul. He believed that individuals create their reality from within, and this proverb aligns with the idea that the inner core of a person is inherently pure and powerful.

- **Sustained Joy through Imagination**: From Goddard's perspective, the soul's sweet delight is a testament to the power of positive imagination and feeling, which can maintain its purity and joy regardless of outer circumstances.

Application to Everyday Life:

- **Cultivating Inner Joy**: Recognize and nurture the inherent joy within, understanding that it remains untainted by external factors. This encourages a focus on inner happiness and fulfillment.

- **Resilience in Adversity**: Remember that the core of your being remains pure and joyful, which can be a source of strength and resilience in difficult times.

- **Appreciating Inner Beauty**: Regularly take time to appreciate

The Alchemy of Vision

the inherent beauty and purity of your own spirit and that of others, fostering a more positive, joyful outlook on life.

Proverb 54: "When thou seest an eagle, thou seest a portion of genius; lift up thy head!"

Analysis:

This proverb speaks to the inspiration and awe that nature can evoke in us, using the eagle, a symbol of freedom and power, as a representative of the larger forces of the world and the genius that resides within them.

Interpretation:

- Eagle as a Symbol: The eagle, soaring high above, epitomizes freedom, vision, and transcendence. Seeing it reminds us of the boundless possibilities and the genius inherent in nature and, by extension, within ourselves.

- Lifting One's Gaze: By encouraging the reader to "lift up thy head," the proverb implies a need to look beyond the mundane and immediate to recognize the grandeur and brilliance of the world.

- Connection to the Divine: The eagle, with its lofty flight, can also symbolize a bridge between the earthly and the divine, suggesting that moments of insight or inspiration are a touch of   divine genius within us.

Neville Goddard's Perspective:

- Manifestation of Inner Beliefs: Goddard believed that everything external is a reflection of our inner beliefs. Seeing an eagle and recognizing the genius in it can be an external manifestation of one's inner acknowledgment of their capabilities and potential.

- Elevation of Consciousness: Just as the eagle soars high, individuals, too, can elevate their consciousness, tapping into the boundless potential within.

Application to Everyday Life:

- Seek Inspiration: Just as the sight of an eagle can inspire, actively seek moments, experiences, or observations in everyday life that uplift and motivate.

- Recognize Inner Potential: Understand that the genius observed in nature is a reflection of the latent genius within each individual. It's a call to recognize and cultivate one's abilities.

- Mindfulness and Perspective: In challenging moments, metaphorically, 'lifting one's head' can provide a fresh perspective, shifting focus from immediate problems to the bigger picture.

The Alchemy of Vision

Proverb 55: "As the caterpillar chooses the fairest leaves to lay her eggs on, so the priest lays his curse on the fairest joys."

Analysis:

This proverb juxtaposes the natural behavior of a caterpillar with the actions of religious authorities, highlighting the potential for suppression of life's purest and most joyful experiences by institutional doctrines.

Interpretation:

- Nature's Selection vs. Religious Suppression: While the caterpillar's choice of the best leaves is driven by an instinctual desire to give its offspring the best start, the priest's "curse" on the finest joys implies the dampening or condemnation of some of life's most genuine pleasures by religious or societal constraints.

- Questioning Dogma: In line with Blake's often skeptical stance on organized religion, this proverb challenges the dogmatic beliefs that sometimes limit human experiences or label them as sinful.

- Preservation vs. Restriction: The caterpillar acts out of preservation and the continuation of life, whereas the priest's actions may stem from control or restriction.

Neville Goddard's Perspective:

- Internal vs. External Authority: Goddard emphasized the internal divine power of imagination and belief. In this light, the "priest" could represent external authorities that limit or dictate one's experience, while the true joys come from internal realization and manifestation.

- Manifestation of Belief: If one believes in the restrictions and curses imposed by external figures, they manifest in one's reality. Conversely, recognizing the divine within can lead to the manifestation of life's purest joys.

Application to Everyday Life:

- Embrace Authentic Experiences: Seek and cherish authentic joys and experiences without letting external dogmas or beliefs overshadow them.

- Question External Authorities: Always question and evaluate any external authority that aims to limit or define what should bring joy or fulfillment.

- Trust in Natural Instincts: Just as the caterpillar instinctively knows where to lay its eggs, trust in personal instincts and feelings when it comes to pursuing joy and satisfaction.

The Alchemy of Vision

Proverb 56: "To create a little flower is the labor of ages."

Analysis:

This proverb underscores the intricacy and depth involved in seemingly simple natural creations, emphasizing that the creation of even the smallest and most delicate things requires vast amounts of time, evolution, and cosmic interplay.

Interpretation:

- Complexity in Simplicity: The "little flower," while appearing simple and delicate, represents the culmination of countless processes and influences spanning vast timescales. Its creation is a testament to the grandeur of natural evolution and cosmic synchronicity.

- Valuing the Insignificant: At a deeper level, the proverb calls attention to the importance of seemingly insignificant things, urging readers to value and appreciate the smaller details of life and the universe.

- The Grandeur of Creation: Everything, no matter how small, is a result of complex processes and should be revered as a manifestation of the universe's vast workings.

Neville Goddard's Perspective:

- Manifestation Takes Time: Just as the creation of a flower involves countless influences over the ages, the manifestation of our desires in the physical world requires time, patience, and the alignment of various forces.

- Appreciation of the Process: The beauty of a flower and the joy of a fulfilled desire are not just in their realization but also in appreciating the intricate processes that lead to their manifestation.

The Alchemy of Vision

Application to Everyday Life:

- Patience in Pursuits: Recognize that valuable outcomes, whether personal growth or achieving goals, often require time, persistence, and an appreciation of the journey.

- Observing Details: Take time to observe and appreciate the finer details of the world around you, understanding the depth and complexity behind each creation.

- Reverence for Life: Value all forms of life and creation, understanding the immense processes that go into their existence.

<u>Proverb 57: "Damn braces. Bless relaxes."</u>

Analysis:

This proverb delves into the duality of condemnation and approval, suggesting that resistance strengthens or awakens while acceptance eases or pacifies.

Interpretation:

- Duality of Emotion: "Damn" and "bless" represent opposing emotional reactions. To "damn" something is to express disapproval, while to "bless" is to approve or wish well.

- Action and Reaction: The act of condemning (bracing) can serve as a motivator or wake-up call, often spurring action or change. Conversely, blessing (relaxing) can provide comfort, ease, and a sense of acceptance.

- Nature of Growth: Challenges, represented by "damn braces," often foster growth and resilience. Blessings, on the other hand, offer solace and rest, allowing for reflection and recuperation.

Neville Goddard's Perspective:

- Emotional Energy in Creation: Goddard would likely interpret "damn braces" as the emotional energy or intensity that drives manifestation. "Bless relaxes" would signify the release of that energy, trusting in the universe to bring forth the desired outcome.

- Power of Feeling: The feeling or emotion behind a desire is crucial in Goddard's teachings. The intensity of condemnation can serve as a potent force in conscious creation, while blessings pave the way for graceful unfoldings.

Application to Everyday Life:

- Harnessing Emotions: Embrace both the challenges and comforts in life. Understand that resistance can serve as a catalyst for growth, while blessings offer opportunities for reflection and gratitude.

The Alchemy of Vision

- Balancing Action and Rest: While it's essential to face challenges head-on and use them as stepping stones, it's equally vital to find moments of relaxation and gratitude to recharge and gain perspective.

- Guided Responses: Instead of reacting impulsively, take a moment to decide whether a situation requires a push (bracing) or acceptance (relaxing) to navigate it effectively.

<u>Proverb 58: "The best wine is the oldest, the best water, the newest."</u>

Analysis:

This proverb contrasts the maturation process of wine with the freshness of water, highlighting the value of both age and immediacy in different contexts.

Interpretation:

- Value of Age: Just as wine improves and becomes richer with age, so too do certain aspects of life, such as wisdom, experience, and relationships.

- Importance of Freshness: Conversely, the freshness of water underscores the need for renewal, rejuvenation, and the appreciation of the present moment in life.

- Balancing Old and New: Life requires a balance between

valuing the aged, accumulated wisdom and embracing the new, immediate experiences.

Neville Goddard's Perspective:

- Age as Imagination's Fruit: Goddard might see the aged wine as the manifestation of one's beliefs and desires, reflecting the fruits of one's imaginative efforts over time.

- Freshness of the Present: The new water would signify the ever-present now, emphasizing the power of the present moment in shaping one's reality.

Application to Everyday Life:

- Respect for Experience: Cherish accumulated experiences and knowledge, for they can serve as a guiding beacon in life.

- Embrace the Present: While it's essential to respect and learn from the past, living in the present and staying open to new experiences is crucial for growth and happiness.

- Versatility in Approach: Understand when to rely on time-tested wisdom and when to be spontaneous and adaptable to the ever-changing circumstances of life.

Proverb 59: "Prayers plow not, praises reap not, joys laugh not, sorrows weep not."

The Alchemy of Vision

Analysis:

This proverb utilizes paradoxical statements to emphasize the limitations of mere words or feelings without action, hinting at the need for genuine effort and understanding.

Interpretation:

- Beyond Surface Actions: The proverb suggests that mere rituals or sentiments, like prayers and praises, are not enough. True spiritual or personal growth requires deeper understanding and actions.

- Contrast in Emotions: The juxtaposition of joys and sorrows showcases life's dualities, emphasizing that mere feelings do not define the entirety of an experience.

- Call for Authenticity: The essence of each statement is a call to move beyond superficial expressions and delve into genuine understanding and effort.

Neville Goddard's Perspective:

- Power of Belief: Goddard would argue that it's not just the act of prayer that matters but the genuine belief and feeling behind it, which shapes our reality.

- Internal Reflection: The distinction between external expressions and internal beliefs is crucial for Goddard. In this proverb, he might see a reflection of the need to align one's internal states with desired outcomes.

Application to Everyday Life:

- Action Over Words: While sentiments and expressions have their place, true progress and understanding require actionable efforts.

- Embrace Genuine Emotions: It's essential to feel and understand one's joys and sorrows deeply rather than merely expressing them.

- Seek Depth: In all aspects of life, whether spirituality, relationships, or personal growth, it's crucial to seek depth and authenticity.

Proverb 60: "The head sublime, the heart pathos, the genitals beauty, the hands and feet proportion."

Analysis:

Blake beautifully delves into the different parts of the human body as representations of various abstract concepts. He underscores the multi-faceted nature of humanity, where each part serves as a metaphor for different aspects of life and perception.

Interpretation:

- The Head - Thought and Aspiration: The use of "sublime"

for the head emphasizes the loftiness of human thought, intellect, and our capacity to aspire for greatness.

- The Heart - Emotion and Experience: "Pathos" symbolizes the depth of human emotion, the capacity for empathy, and the richness of our experiences.

- The Genitals - Creation and Aesthetics: Associating them with "beauty" highlights the human ability for creation, not just biologically, but also in terms of art, culture, and other expressions.

- The Hands and Feet - Action and Journey: "Proportion" could be interpreted as balance and movement, indicating that our actions (hands) and our journey through life (feet) should be measured and balanced.

Neville Goddard's Perspective:

- Manifestation and Creation: The reference to different body parts might be viewed by Goddard as symbolic of how we manifest our realities. The head (imagination), the heart (feeling), and the genitals (creation) can be viewed as the process of bringing desires into reality.

- Balanced Living: The mention of hands and feet stresses the importance of grounded actions and movements in harmony with one's desires and beliefs.

Application to Everyday Life:

- Holistic Understanding: Recognizing the intrinsic value of each part of ourselves, not just physically but symbolically, can lead to a more integrated and holistic approach to life.

- Balance in Action and Feeling: Emphasizing proportion, the proverb serves as a reminder to ensure balance in our actions, emotions, and aspirations.

- Celebrate Creation and Beauty: Recognizing the beauty in creation and the aesthetics of life can lead to a richer appreciation of everyday experiences.

<u>Proverb 61: "As the air to a bird, or the sea to a fish, so is contempt to the contemptible."</u>

Analysis:

Through this proverb, Blake underscores the innate nature of things and the inevitability of reactions based on intrinsic qualities. Just as birds are suited for air and fish for water, contemptible actions or behaviors naturally attract disdain.

Interpretation:

- Natural Habitat and Consequence: Just as a bird naturally thrives in the air and a fish in the sea, individuals who display contemptible behaviors naturally find themselves in a realm

The Alchemy of Vision

of contempt.

- **Reflection of Inner Nature:** The outer world often mirrors one's inner nature. Thus, if one projects contemptible traits, they will inevitably be met with contempt from the world around.

- **Inevitability of Reaction:** Certain actions, behaviors, or attitudes naturally elicit specific reactions, and there's a certain inescapability to this dynamic.

Neville Goddard's Perspective:

- **External Reflection of Inner Belief:** Goddard would likely interpret this as a reflection of the belief that our external world mirrors our internal state. If one holds contemptible beliefs about themselves or others, they'll manifest experiences that reflect those beliefs.

- **Natural Flow of Consciousness:** Just as it's natural for a bird to be in the air or a fish in the sea, it's natural for our beliefs to manifest in our reality.

Application to Everyday Life:

- **Self-awareness:** It's crucial to be aware of the energy and behaviors we project, as they play a significant role in the reactions and situations we encounter.

- Mindfulness: To change our external experiences, we must first address and adjust our internal beliefs and attitudes.

- Acceptance of Consequences: Understanding that our actions have reactions, often mirroring the nature of our deeds, can lead to more thoughtful choices.

Proverb 62: The crow wished everything was black; to the owl, that everything was white."

The Alchemy of Vision

Analysis:

This proverb delves into the realm of perspective and subjectivity, suggesting that individuals view the world through the lens of their own experiences, preferences, and inclinations. Just as the crow may prefer the color black and the owl white, humans often project their desires onto the world around them.

Interpretation:

- Subjectivity of Perception: The crow's preference for black and the owl's for white serve as metaphors for the unique ways in which individuals perceive and interpret their surroundings.

- Bias and Projection: Just as the crow and owl have biases towards certain colors, humans too possess biases, often projecting them onto situations or people.

- Diversity of Vision: While it's natural to have personal preferences, it's essential to recognize that they are merely individual perspectives amidst a vast spectrum of viewpoints.

Neville Goddard's Perspective:

- Creation Through Belief: In line with Goddard's teachings, our beliefs shape our reality. If one firmly believes in a particular viewpoint (black for the crow, white for the owl), then their experiences will align with that belief.

- Subjective Realities: Each individual creates a unique reality based on their inner convictions and desires.

Application to Everyday Life:

- Embracing Different Perspectives: While it's okay to have personal preferences and views, it's beneficial to remain open to diverse perspectives, understanding that others might see things differently.

- Self-awareness: Recognize and acknowledge our biases and work towards understanding where they stem from. This introspection can lead to growth and a broader worldview.

- Celebrate Diversity: Just as the crow and owl have their color preferences, humans, too, have varied experiences, beliefs, and values. By celebrating these differences, we can cultivate a more inclusive and understanding society.

The Alchemy of Vision

Proverb 63: "Exuberance is beauty."

Analysis:

This proverb celebrates the vibrant, overflowing energy of life, suggesting that there's beauty in passion, enthusiasm, and an uninhibited expression of joy. Exuberance, in its uncontrolled and spontaneous form, can be more genuine and alluring than calculated or restrained beauty.

Interpretation:

- Vibrancy of Life: Exuberance encapsulates the essence of life in its most vivid and dynamic form, where raw emotion and energy are put forth without reservations.

- Uninhibited Expression: Beauty isn't just about symmetry or accepted standards; it's also found in the spontaneous outburst of emotions, be it joy, love, or even sorrow.

- Challenging Conventional Beauty: Traditional definitions of beauty often involve restraint and conformity. Blake, in his typical fashion, challenges this notion, proposing that raw, unfiltered emotion is equally, if not more, beautiful.

Neville Goddard's Perspective:

- Joy in Creation: Goddard would likely view exuberance as the ecstatic expression that arises when one's desires and imaginations manifest in reality.

- Embracing Life's Fullness: For Goddard, understanding one's power of imagination and its implications on reality can lead to an exuberant state, embracing the beauty of life's potential.

Application to Everyday Life:

- Celebrate Passion: Embrace and celebrate moments of

strong emotion and passion in oneself and others, recognizing the beauty in such genuine expressions.

- Redefining Beauty: Instead of adhering strictly to societal standards of beauty, consider expanding one's definition to include raw emotion and passion.

- Live Fully: Approach life with enthusiasm and energy, understanding that these moments of unbridled joy and emotion are beautiful in their right.

Proverb 64: "If the lion was advised by the Fox, he would be cunning."

Analysis:

This proverb explores the interplay of innate nature and external influences. The lion, symbolizing strength and courage, and the fox, representing cunning and craftiness, together highlight that our core attributes can be altered or enhanced by the wisdom or traits of others.

Interpretation:

- Interchange of Traits: While the lion inherently possesses strength and nobility, the proverb implies that absorbing the fox's cunning would make him even more formidable.

- Value of Counsel: Even the most powerful and independent

entities can benefit from the advice of those with different skill sets.

- Identity and Influence: While one's essence remains, it can be influenced and even enhanced by external factors.

Neville Goddard's Perspective:

- Inner and Outer Reality: Goddard might view the lion as representing our inherent strengths and the fox as external influences or beliefs. By blending our innate qualities with learned strategies, we can manifest a more robust reality.

- Harmonious Integration: Embracing both strength (lion) and cunning (fox) ensures a balanced approach to manifesting our desires.

Application to Everyday Life:

- Embrace Diversity: Recognize the value of seeking advice or opinions from those with different perspectives or strengths.

- Enhance Innate Abilities: While it's essential to acknowledge and harness one's natural strengths, it's equally crucial to be open to learning and incorporating new strategies.

- Collaboration Over Competition: Rather than viewing others solely as competition, consider the potential of collaborative efforts that combine various strengths.

Proverb 65: "Improvements make straight roads, but the crooked roads without improvement are roads of genius."

Analysis:

This proverb contrasts the structured, planned progression with the unpredictable, unstructured path of original thought and creativity. It alludes to the idea that while there is merit in refining and optimizing, there is also innate value in the untouched, organic, and untamed.

Interpretation:

- Structured vs. Organic Progress: "Straight roads" imply systematic, planned progress, while "crooked roads" suggest natural, undirected growth. Both have their significance.

- Originality Over Refinement: While improvements and enhancements are valuable, there's an inherent genius in the raw, original ideas and paths.

- Embracing Imperfection: The proverb encourages us to see the beauty and wisdom in the imperfect, winding routes of life.

Neville Goddard's Perspective:

- Manifestation Paths: Goddard might perceive the straight roads as the direct manifestations of our conscious desires, while the crooked roads represent the unpredictable yet magical ways the subconscious brings our desires to fruition.

- Value of the Journey: The unpredictable, non-linear path can often lead to the most profound realizations and manifestations, emphasizing the idea that the journey is as vital as the destination.

Application to Everyday Life:

- Honor Your Path: Whether you're taking a methodical approach to life or navigating its twists and turns, recognize the value in your journey.

- Innovation and Creativity: While there's a place for optimization and refinement, don't forget to value and nurture raw creativity and original thought.

- Celebrate Diversity of Experience: Understand that every individual's path is unique. Embrace and learn from the varied journeys of those around you.

Proverb 66: "Sooner murder an infant in its cradle than nurse unacted desires."

The Alchemy of Vision

Analysis:

This provocative proverb speaks to the consequences of suppressing our true desires and instincts. By using the shocking image of an infant's murder, Blake draws attention to the severe repercussions of neglecting our innate passions and yearnings.

Interpretation:

- The Dangers of Repression: The proverb warns of the detrimental effects of stifling one's genuine desires. When one's innermost passions are neglected, it can lead to inner turmoil, much like the harm caused by committing such a heinous act.

- Inherent Urgency: The intensity of the imagery underscores the importance of acting upon one's true feelings and instincts without delay.

- Authenticity vs. Societal Expectations: Society often expects us to suppress or modify our true desires to fit within cultural norms. Blake challenges this notion, urging us to honor our genuine selves.

Neville Goddard's Perspective:

- Power of Desires: For Goddard, desires are not merely wishes but divine hints of what's possible. Not acting upon them is equivalent to denying the universe's offering.

- Manifestation: Suppressed desires can't manifest into reality. By nurturing and acting upon our desires, we align with the universe's plan for us, allowing our dreams to materialize.

Application to Everyday Life:

- Honor Your Truth: Recognize and accept your true passions and desires without judgment. Understand that these feelings are a crucial part of who you are.

- Take Action: Don't just acknowledge your desires; act upon them. Even if it's a small step, moving forward aligns you with your purpose.

- Avoid Regret: Suppressed desires can lead to a life of regret. Embrace your true self and live authentically to experience a fulfilled life.

Proverb 67: "Where man is not, nature is barren."

Analysis:

This proverb delves into the interconnected relationship between man and nature, highlighting the influence and significance of human presence and perception on the richness of the natural world.

Interpretation:

- Nature's Value Through Human Perception: While nature

exists independently, its beauty, depth, and richness might be fully realized only when observed or experienced by humans. This viewpoint suggests that man brings meaning to nature.

- Nature's Reliance on Human Care: The proverb could also indicate that without human cultivation or care, nature could turn unproductive or desolate, emphasizing the stewardship role humans play.

- Interdependence: At a deeper level, the proverb may underline the symbiotic relationship between humans and nature. Neither is truly complete without the other.

Neville Goddard's Perspective:

- Conscious Creation: Goddard would likely interpret this in the realm of consciousness and creation. In his teachings, the external world (including nature) mirrors our internal beliefs. In this light, nature's "barrenness" could mean the lack of imaginative input from humans.

- Power of Observation: For Goddard, the act of observation and imagination gives life meaning. Nature's fullness might be realized through the consciousness of man.

Application to Everyday Life:

- Appreciate Nature's Beauty: Take the time to observe, experience, and reflect on the natural world around you. Your appreciation adds richness to it.

- Stewardship: Recognize your role in taking care of the environment. Your actions, big or small, contribute to the health and productivity of nature.

- Seek Harmony: Endeavor to live in harmony with nature, recognizing that both humans and the natural world benefit from a balanced relationship.

<u>Proverb 68: "Truth can never be told so as to be understood, and not be believed."</u>

Analysis:

This proverb delves into the essence of truth, its inherent power, and the undeniable impact it has when genuinely grasped.

Interpretation:

- Inherent Conviction of Truth: When the truth is presented in a manner that can be truly comprehended, it carries an undeniable force that compels belief. It implies that genuine understanding is intrinsically linked with belief.

- Barrier of Complexity: Sometimes, the truth is obscured or complex. When simplified or articulated clearly, its acceptance becomes almost inevitable.

- Societal Skepticism: At another layer, this might be a commentary on the skepticism of society. Truth, when not understood, might be disregarded, but once it's understood, its power is undeniable.

Neville Goddard's Perspective:

- Inner Convictions: Goddard would relate truth to inner convictions and imagination. For him, when one understands their personal truth or desire and feels it in their imagination, it's bound to manifest in their reality.

- Power of Assumption: Goddard emphasized assuming the feeling of the wish fulfilled. This proverb aligns with his teachings; when one understands and assumes their truth, it's believed and manifested.

Application to Everyday Life:

- Seek Clarity: In conversations and debates, strive for clarity. When truths are understood, they have a better chance of being believed and accepted.

- Trust Your Intuition: When something resonates as true for you, trust that intuition. Often, our inner selves recognize truths before our conscious minds can articulate them.

- Educate with Simplicity: When imparting knowledge or truths, aim for simplicity and clarity to ensure understanding and acceptance.

Proverb 69: "Enough! Or too much."

Analysis:

This succinct proverb confronts the delicate balance between sufficiency and excess, probing the boundaries of satisfaction and indulgence.

Interpretation:

- Fine Line Between Sufficiency and Excess: Life often teeters between what's just right and what's overboard. Recognizing when something is "enough" can prevent the pitfalls of "too much."

- Materialism and Desire: In a world driven by consumption, the proverb nudges individuals to assess what they truly need versus what they want out of sheer desire or societal influence.

- Intuitive Balance: At its core, the proverb is a call for intuition and self-awareness, prompting individuals to discern the tipping point between fulfillment and gluttony.

The Alchemy of Vision

Neville Goddard's Perspective:

- Desires and Manifestation: Goddard might see this proverb as a reflection on the nature of desires. While desires are natural and can be manifested, unchecked desires can lead to a sense of constant longing or even negative manifestations.

- Contentment in Creation: There's power in understanding and being content with our manifestations. Constantly seeking more might lead to a never-ending cycle of dissatisfaction.

Application to Everyday Life:

- Mindful Consumption: Whether it's material goods, information, or even emotions, it's essential to consume mindfully and recognize when you've reached a point of satisfaction.

- Self-awareness: Regularly check in with yourself. Are you seeking something out of genuine need, or is it a mere pursuit of excess?

- Celebrate Sufficiency: Recognize and celebrate moments of "enough." Gratitude for what one has can lead to a richer, more fulfilling life.

Conclusion:

As we reflect upon the teachings of William Blake and Neville Goddard, it's evident that their union is not a mere coincidence of thought but a profound alignment of vision. While Blake painted a universe with words and images, Goddard provided the tools to navigate it.

This union of visionaries beckons each of us to embark on our own journey of exploration, to challenge our perceptions, to embrace our imaginative power, and to realize the profound truth that within us lies the potential to shape our reality.

In this ever-evolving dance of existence, may the combined wisdom of Blake and Goddard serve as a guiding light, illuminating the path toward deeper understanding, boundless creativity, and unparalleled transformation. In their union, we find the promise of our own limitless potential.

The thing that hath been, it is that which shall be; and that which is done is that which shall be done: and there is NO new thing under the sun." (Eccl. 1:9)

Acknowledgment

There are names in our lives that become synonymous with love, support, and unwavering faith. These are the names that have held my hand, been my compass, and steadied my ship during tumultuous seas.

To my mother, Nancy, and sister, Laura: Your constant presence and ceaseless love have been the bedrock upon which I've built my life. You've been there during my highs and lows, standing beside me when the world seemed an overwhelming place. The depth of my gratitude for you both is beyond words.

To my radiant daughters, Ellery and Tillie K: You have both been my anchors and my inspiration. Sharing my learnings with you and watching you grow and absorb the world with such intelligence and grace has been one of my greatest joys. I understand the challenges of adapting to the constant evolution of a parent; your resilience and understanding, despite my often complex metamorphosis, have been nothing short of extraordinary. I am incredibly proud to call you my daughters.

And to Lynn: Our time together may be measured in mere months compared to years, but your impact on my life is immeasurable. Your love, support, and, sometimes, sacrifices – both emotional and financial – have been instrumental in bringing this book to life. Thank you for seeing the best in me, even when I struggled to see it in myself.

To each one of you, I owe a debt of gratitude that words can hardly express. You have been the mirror reflecting my true self, ensuring I never lose sight of who I am and who I strive to be. This book might carry my name, but its spirit, its essence, is a testament to the love and unwavering support of each one of you.

Thank you from the depths of my heart.

MYCHAEL T. RENN

About The Author

With a diverse tapestry of experiences, spanning law-enforcement, a deep dive into the world of psychedelics, and an immersive journey through the craft of welding. The authors path has been one of both physical and metaphysical exploration. Emerging as a patrol officer in 2001 his time and law-enforcement became a lens through which human behavior and society were analyzed, from routine patrols to investigating clandestine laboratories. These experiences primed the foundation for alchemical transformation the trajectory led beyond, to an endeavor that melded the practical with the profound, a union welder for over 15 years. In the searing glow of welding arts, metals fused into unity a mirroring the alchemical synthesis of elements. Hands at once shaped steel soon sculpted insights, weaving, a seekers journey.

A profound odyssey into the realms of psychedelic served as another facet of transformation no less than 15 ego deaths on psychedelic mushrooms and countless explorations within DMT like domains and a remarkable month-long voyage, guided by LSD their profound encounters illuminated the concealed corners of consciousness. Through the prism of experience and introspection, the author crafted *"The alchemy of Vision."* This work harmonizes past wisdom, creating a unified exploration of both heaven and hells depths. This book stands as a testament to the alchemy of life a-synthesis of experiences forging an ever evolving philosopher, a writer of ideas, and explorer of realms, both seen and unseen.

Be sure to look for my upcoming publications, *"Nailed It, A Metaphysical Translation of Bible Parables,"* and *"The Alchemy of the Soul: The Metamorphosis from Base to Divine- Facing our inner Demons in the Pseudomonarchia Daemonum."*